A Basic Bibliographic Guide
for
New Testament Exegesis

# A Basic Bibliographic Guide for New Testament Exegesis

*by*

**DAVID M. SCHOLER**

Second Edition

WILLIAM B. EERDMANS PUBLISHING COMPANY
Grand Rapids, Michigan

First Edition, South Hamilton, Massachusetts:
Gordon-Conwell Bookcentre, 1971
Second Edition © 1973 by David M. Scholer
Library of Congress Catalog Card Number 72-94610
ISBN 0-8028-1503-0
Printed in the United States of America

*Reprinted, December 1978*

*To*

*WILLIAM L. LANE*
*and*
*J. RAMSEY MICHAELS*

*my former teachers*
*and present colleagues*

# Contents

# Introduction

The purpose of this bibliographic guide is to assist the theological student and seminary-educated person to do the exegetical task of interpreting the New Testament and to build an adequate and reliable personal library in the area of New Testament studies. For the latter reason in particular, books have been suggested (and generally ones in print) to the virtual exclusion of articles.

Clearly there is no attempt to be exhaustive; rather the emphasis is on selectivity with very brief annotations. Savants in New Testament studies will miss many important titles in German and French especially. However, the average seminarian or seminary graduate in this country does not use these languages, and thus such works are not included here. Where both British and American editions of a work exist, usually only the American publisher is listed.

It will be equally clear to all users of this guide that it is limited to books that have appeared in English by mid-1972. This will be substantially adequate for most areas for some time; those using this guide in a classroom context will know how to supplement it as new items of value appear.

This guide had a predecessor several years ago at Gordon Divinity School in a classroom syllabus prepared by J. Ramsey Michaels. Although I am indebted to him for the initial inspiration for the project, this guide is a totally new work and my responsibility alone.

Several people have made suggestions for this guide, and to all of them I am indebted. I wish to thank the editors of the William B. Eerdmans Publishing Company for their prompt and helpful manner in accepting this work for publication. The typing for the first edition was done by Margaret Anderson, revisions were typed by Sylvia Lloyd, and Gail Crowell typed the final manuscript. I appreciate their work and that of my wife Jeannette in preparing the author index.

David M. Scholer
*Assistant Professor of New Testament*
*Gordon-Conwell Theological Seminary*
*South Hamilton, Massachusetts 01982*

August 31, 1972

Chapter One

# Other Bibliographic Surveys

There are, of course, other guides listing tools for biblical study that are useful and may be consulted in conjunction with this guide:

1.1　F. W. Danker, *Multipurpose Tools for Bible Study* (3rd ed.; St. Louis: Concordia, 1970);

1.2　G. S. Glanzman and J. A. Fitzmyer, *An Introductory Bibliography for the Study of Scripture* (Woodstock Papers No. 5; Westminster: Newman, 1961); and

1.3　B. H. Kelly and D. G. Miller, *Tools for Bible Study* (Richmond: John Knox, 1956).

The work of Danker is especially useful because of its extensive discussions of the background and nature of many of the bibliographic tools of exegesis. For that reason it will be cited at appropriate points throughout this guide.

Other bibliographic surveys of a more general nature are:

1.4　*A Bibliographical Guide to New Testament Research* (The Tyndale Fellowship for Biblical Research; Cambridge: Tyndale House, 1968);

1.5　*A Bibliography of Bible Study for Theological Students* (2nd ed.; Princeton Seminary Pamphlets No. 1; Princeton: Princeton Theological Seminary, 1960);

1.6 *Theological Bibliographies: Essential Books for a Minister's Library* (*Andover Newton Quarterly* 4 [1963]); *1964-1966 Supplement* (*Andover Newton Quarterly* 6 [1966], suppl.);

1.7 C. E. Armerding and W. W. Gasque, "A Bibliography for Christians," *Christianity Today* 15 (1970/71), 122-25, 273-75, 449-50, 797-99; 16 (1971/72), 353-56; 402-04; 17 (1972/73), 74-79 (to be cont.); and

1.8 H. D. Merchant, *Encounter with Books: A Guide to Christian Reading* (Downers Grove: Inter-Varsity, 1970), 1-6, 15-22, 25-28, 31-33.

A fairly useful library guide for theological research is:

1.9 E. V. Aldrich and T. E. Camp, *Using Theological Books and Libraries* (Englewood Cliffs: Prentice-Hall, 1963).

Chapter Two

# Bibliographic Tools

The most general and comprehensive guide to bibliographies for New Testament studies is:

2.1 J. C. Hurd, Jr., *A Bibliography of New Testament Bibliographies* (New York: Seabury, 1966).

There are several special bibliographies on New Testament texts and topics (some of which are mentioned in Hurd):

2.2 B. M. Metzger, *Index of Articles on the New Testament and the Early Church Published in Festschriften* (Journal of Biblical Literature Monograph Series, Vol. V; Philadelphia: Society of Biblical Literature, 1951) with *Supplement* (1955)—covers through 1950;

2.3 B. M. Metzger, *Annotated Bibliography of the Textual Criticism of the New Testament 1914-1939* (Studies and Documents XVI; Copenhagen: Ejnar Munksgaard, 1955);

2.4 D. Y. Hadidian, *A Periodical and Monographic Index to the Literature on the Gospels and Acts based on the files of the École Biblique in Jerusalem* (Bibliographia Tripotamopolitana, No. 3; Pittsburgh: The Clifford E. Barbour Library, Pittsburgh Theological Seminary, 1971);

2.5     B. M. Metzger, *Index to Periodical Literature on Christ and the Gospels* (New Testament Tools and Studies, Vol. VI; Leiden: E. J. Brill/Grand Rapids: Wm. B. Eerdmans, 1966)—covers through 1961;

2.6     E. Malatesta, *St. John's Gospel 1920-1965: A Cumulative and Classified Bibliography of Book and Periodical Literature on the Fourth Gospel* (Analecta Biblica 32; Rome: Pontifical Biblical Institute, 1967);

2.7     A. J. Mattill, Jr. and M. B. Mattill, *A Classified Bibliography of Literature on the Acts of the Apostles* (New Testament Tools and Studies, Vol. VII; Leiden: E. J. Brill/Grand Rapids: Wm. B. Eerdmans, 1966)—covers through 1961;

2.8     B. M. Metzger, *Index to Periodical Literature on the Apostle Paul* (New Testament Tools and Studies, Vol. I; Leiden: E. J. Brill/Grand Rapids: Wm. B. Eerdmans, 1960)—covers through 1957; and

2.9     C. Ghidelli, "Bibliographia Biblica Petrina," *Scuola Cattolica* 96 (1968), 62*-110* (see *New Testament Abstracts* 13:91).

There are several special bibliographies on topics and texts in the areas of New Testament backgrounds. The bibliographies in the area of Judaism are:

2.10    G. Delling, *Bibliographie zur jüdischen-hellenistischen und intertestamentarischen Literatur 1900-1965* (Texte und Untersuchungen, Band 106; Berlin: Akademie-Verlag, 1969);

2.11    C. Burchard, *Bibliographie zu den Handschriften vom Toten Meer* (Beihefte zur Zeitschrift für die Alttestamentliche Wissenschaft 76; Berlin: Alfred Töpelmann, 1959);

2.12    C. Burchard, *Bibliographie zu den Handschriften vom Toten Meer: II NR. 1557-4459* (Beihefte zur Zeitschrift für die Alttestamentliche Wissenschaft 89; Berlin: Alfred Töpelmann, 1965)—these two bibliographies on the Dead Sea Scrolls are continued in the periodical *Revue de Qumran;*

2.13   B. Jongeling, *A Classified Bibliography of the Finds in the Desert of Judah 1958-1969* (Studies on the Texts of the Desert of Judah, Vol. VII; Leiden: E. J. Brill, 1971);

2.14   W. S. LaSor, *Bibliography of the Dead Sea Scrolls 1948-1957* (Fuller Theological Seminary Bibliographical Series No. 2; Pasadena: Fuller Theological Seminary Library, 1958);

2.15   M. Yizhar, *Bibliography of Hebrew Publications on the Dead Sea Scrolls 1948-1964* (Harvard Theological Studies XXIII; Cambridge: Harvard University Press, 1967);

2.16   L. H. Feldman, *Studies in Judaica: Scholarship on Philo and Josephus (1937-1962)* (New York: Yeshiva University, n.d.)— (corrections noted in *Studia Philonica* 1 [1972], 56);

2.17   E. Hilgert, "A Bibliography of Philo Studies, 1963-1970," *Studia Philonica* 1 (1972), 57-71;

2.18   H. Schreckenberg, *Bibliographie zu Flavius Josephus* (Arbeiten zur Literatur und Geschichte des hellenistischen Judentums I; Leiden: E. J. Brill, 1968);

2.19   P. Nickels, *Targum and New Testament: A Bibliography together with a New Testament Index* (Scripta Pontificii Instituti Biblici 117; Rome: Pontifical Biblical Institute, 1967);

2.20   C. Berlin, *Index to Festschriften in Jewish Studies* (New York: Ktav, 1971);

2.21   L. A. Mayer, *A Bibliography of the Samaritans* (ed. D. Broadribb; Suppl. to Abr-Nahrain I; Leiden: E. J. Brill, 1964); and

2.22   R. Weiss, *Select Bibliography on the Samari-*

15

tans: *The Samaritans and the Samaritan Text of the Torah* (2nd ed.; Jerusalem: Academon, 1970).

For bibliography on the Graeco-Roman Hellenistic world there are (see also 2.36):

2.23 N. J. Burich, *Alexander the Great: A Bibliography* (Kent: Kent State University Press, 1970);

2.24 S. Lambrino, *Bibliographie de l'antiquité classique 1896-1914; Première Partie: Auteurs et textes* (Collection de Bibliographie Classique I; Paris: Société d'Édition "Les Belles Lettres," 1951);

2.25 J. Marouzeau, *Dix années de bibliographie classique: Bibliographie critique et analytique de l'antiquité greco-latine pour la période 1914-1924; Première Partie: Auteurs et textes; Deuxiemè Partie: Matières et disciplines* (Collection de Bibliographie Classique II; Paris: Société d'Édition "Les Belles Lettres," 1927-28; repr. 1969); and

2.26 D. Rounds, *Articles on Antiquity in Festschriften: The Ancient Near East; The Old Testament; Greece; Rome; Roman Law; Byzantium* (Cambridge: Harvard University Press, 1962) covers through 1954.

For patristic literature the following is available (see also 2.35; 2.36):

2.27 J. L. Stewardson, *A Bibliography of Bibliographies on Patristics* (Evanston: Garrett Theological Seminary Library, 1967).

Some special topics in the early church are covered in the following:

2.28 A. A. De Marco, *The Tomb of Saint Peter: A Representative and Annotated Bibliography of the Excavations* (Suppl. to Novum Testamentum, Vol. VIII; Leiden: E. J. Brill, 1964);

2.29 D. M. Scholer, *Nag Hammadi Bibliography 1948-1969* (Nag Hammadi Studies, Vol. I; Leiden: E. J. Brill, 1971/Grand Rapids: Wm. B. Eerdmans, 1972); continued in *Novum Testamentum* 13 (1971), 322-36;

2.30 H. Crouzel, *Bibliographie critique d'Origène* (Instrumenta Patristica VIII; Steenbrugis: In Abbatia Sancti Petri/Hagae: Martinus Nijhoff, 1971); and

2.31 R. Farina, *Bibliografia Origeniana 1960-1970* (Biblioteca del "Salesianum" 77; Torino: Società Editrice Internazionale, 1971).

There are several bibliographic periodicals and annuals that are very important for New Testament studies:

2.32 *Elenchus Bibliographicus Biblicus*, published in the periodical *Biblica* beginning in 1920 and published separately beginning with Vol. 49 (1968)—this is the most comprehensive biblical bibliography covering books, reviews and articles in the areas of the Old Testament, New Testament, intertestamental Judaism and the early patristic period;

2.33 *New Testament Abstracts*, Vol. 1 (1956/57) and continuing—this excellent publication, published three times a year, gives a listing of all articles on the New Testament published in over 250 periodicals and provides an abstract in English of each one;

2.34 *Internationale Zeitschriftenschau für Bibelwissenschaft und Grenzgebiete*, Vol. 1 (1951/52) and continuing—this lists biblical articles and provides abstracts in German;

2.35 *Bibliographia Patristica*, Vol. 1 for 1956 (1959) and continuing—this lists books, reviews and articles for the patristic period; and

2.36 *L'Année Philologique*, Vol. 1 (1924) and continuing—this lists books, reviews and articles on subjects in antiquity and is especially valuable for topics in Graeco-Roman and Hellenistic history and thought and for its listing of Greek and Latin authors both pagan and patristic (see also 2.24; 2.25).

Chapter Three

# Texts of the New Testament

For general study of any New Testament passage the following two editions of the Greek text should be used:

3.1 E. Nestle and K. Aland, *Novum Testamentum Graece* (25th ed.; Stuttgart: Württembergische Bibelanstalt, 1963) and

3.2 K. Aland, M. Black, C. M. Martini, B. M. Metzger and A. Wikgren in cooperation with the Institute for New Testament Textual Research, *The Greek New Testament* (2nd ed.; United Bible Societies, 1968); available bound together with B. M. Newman, Jr., *A Concise Greek-English Dictionary of the New Testament* (London: United Bible Societies, 1971).

Occasionally more comprehensive editions of the Greek text must be consulted in order to obtain fuller textual evidence. The major such editions are:

3.3 C. Tischendorf, *Novum Testamentum Graece...*, Editio octava critica maior (2 vols.; Lipsiae: Giesecke & Devrient, 1869-72);

3.4 H. F. von Soden, *Das Schriften des Neuen Testaments in ihrer ältesten erreichbaren Textgestalt hergestellt auf Grund ihrer Textgeschichte;* II. Teil: *Text mit Apparat* (Göttingen: Vandenhoeck & Ruprecht, 1913); and

3.5    S. C. E. Legg, *Novum Testamentum Graece secundum Westcotto-Hortianum: Evangelium secundum Marcum cum apparata novo plenissimo* . . . (Oxford: Clarendon, 1935); . . . *Evangelium secundum Matthaeum* . . . (Oxford: Clarendon, 1940).

Data on these major editions, as well as on numerous other editions of the Greek text and on New Testament textual criticism, can be found in the excellent and thorough study of B. M. Metzger:

3.6    B. M. Metzger, *The Text of the New Testament: Its Transmission, Corruption, and Restoration* (2nd ed.; New York and Oxford: Oxford University Press, 1968).

The study of text-critical problems is greatly advanced with the preparation of the volume that gives the rationale for all of the textual decisions made in the United Bible Societies' edition of the New Testament text (3.2; note that the third edition mentioned in the title of the following has not yet appeared):

3.7    B. M. Metzger, *A Textual Commentary on the Greek New Testament: A Companion Volume to the United Bible Societies' Greek New Testament (third edition)* (London and New York: United Bible Societies, 1971 [appeared 1972] ).

For the study of the gospels, particularly the synoptics, the best edition of gospel parallels should be used:

3.8    K. Aland, *Synopsis Quattuor Evangeliorum: Locis parallelis evangeliorum apocryphorum et patrum adhibitus edidit* (6th ed.; Stuttgart: Württembergische Bibelanstalt, 1969).

This edition (3.8) has appeared in a format that will be very helpful to many. The newer format has the same Greek text and textual apparatus as the earlier edition, with an English translation (Revised Standard Version) on facing pages arranged in the same paragraph structure as the Greek text and with some notes on alternative English translations. This newer format does, however, omit the excellent collection of apocryphal and patristic parallels, as well as the collection of Greek and Latin patristic witnesses to the gospels and the translations of the Coptic Gospel of Thomas, included in the earlier edition. The newer format is:

3.9 K. Aland, *Synopsis of the Four Gospels: Greek-English Edition of the Synopsis Quattuor Evangeliorum with the Text of the Revised Standard Version* (United Bible Societies, 1972).

Still of some value are two other English gospel synopses:

3.10 H. F. D. Sparks, *A Synopsis of the Gospels: The Synoptic Gospels with Johannine Parallels* (Philadelphia: Fortress, 1964) and

3.11 B. H. Throckmorton, Jr., *Gospel Parallels: A Synopsis of the First Three Gospels . . .* (3rd ed.; Camden: Thomas Nelson, 1967).

Chapter Four

# Texts of the Old Testament

The New Testament student will often need to examine carefully passages and/or terms in the Old Testament.

The standard critical edition of the Hebrew text is:

4.1   R. Kittel and P. Kahle, *Biblia Hebraica* (14th ed.; Stuttgart: Württembergische Bibelanstalt, 1966).

The standard edition of the Septuagint is:

4.2   A. Rahlfs, *Septuagint, id est, Vetus Testamentum Graece iuxta LXX interpretes* (2 vols.; 8th ed.; Stuttgart: Württembergische Bibelanstalt, 1965).

Also useful for the study of the Septuagint is:

4.3   H. B. Swete, *The Old Testament in Greek According to the Septuagint* (3 vols.; 2nd ed.; Cambridge: University Press, 1895-99).

Some will also find an edition of the Septuagint with an accompanying English translation helpful:

4.4   *The Septuagint Version of the Old Testament, with an English Translation; and with Various Readings and Critical Notes* (Grand Rapids: Zondervan, 1970; repr. of the Samuel Bagster & Sons ed.).

There are two major critical editions of the Septuagint that must often be consulted. Both editions are multi-volumed and neither covers the entire Old Testament. These are the so-called "Cambridge" and "Göttingen" Septuagints:

4.5 A. E. Brooke, N. McLean and H. St. J. Thackeray, *The Old Testament in Greek According to the Text of Codex Vaticanus, Supplemented from Other Uncial Manuscripts, with a Critical Apparatus Containing the Variants of the Chief Ancient Authorities for the Text of the Septuagint* (Cambridge: University Press, 1906-40):

Vol. I,    Part I  :  Genesis (1906)
            Part II  :  Exodus and Leviticus (1909)
            Part III:  Numbers and Deuteronomy (1911)
            Part IV:  Joshua, Judges and Ruth (1917)

Vol. II,   Part I  :  I and II Samuel (1927)
            Part II  :  I and II Kings (1930)
            Part III:  I and II Chronicles (1932)
            Part IV:  I Esdras and Ezra-Nehemiah (1935)

Vol. III,  Part I  :  Esther, Judith and Tobit (1940); and

4.6 *Septuaginta: Vetus Testamentum Graecum auctoritate Societatis Litterarum Gottingensis editum* (Göttingen: Vandenhoeck & Ruprecht, 1931-    ):

VIII.3   Esther (R. Hanhart, 1966)
IX.1     1 Maccabees (W. Kappler, 1936; 2nd ed., 1967)
IX.2     2 Maccabees (W. Kappler and R. Hanhart, 1959)
IX.3     3 Maccabees (R. Hanhart, 1960)
X        Psalmi cum Odis (A. Rahlfs, 1931; 2nd ed., 1967)
XII.1    Sapienta Salomonis (J. Ziegler, 1943)
XII.2    Sapienta Iesu Filii Sirach (J. Ziegler, 1965)
XIII     Duodecim Prophetae (J. Ziegler, 1943; 2nd ed., 1967)

| XIV | Isaias (J. Ziegler, 1939; 2nd ed., 1967) |
| XV | Ieremias, Baruch, Threni, Epistula Ieremiae (J. Ziegler, 1957) |
| XVI.1 | Ezechiel (J. Ziegler, 1952; 2nd ed., 1967) |
| XVI.2 | Susanna, Daniel, Bel et Draco (J. Ziegler, 1954). |

For other Greek versions of the Old Testament the most complete collection remains:

> 4.7 F. Field, *Origenis Hexaplorum quae supersunt; sive veterum interpretum Graecorum in totum Vetus Testamentum fragmenta* ... (2 vols.; Oxford: Clarendon, 1875).

The textual situation of both the Hebrew and Greek Old Testaments is very complex and under considerable discussion by Old Testament textual scholars. No single handbook collects all of the pertinent evidence and textual readings not found in the critical editions cited. The following presentations will give an adequate introduction:

> 4.8 F. M. Cross, Jr., "The Contribution of the Qumran Discoveries to the Study of the Biblical Text," *Israel Exploration Journal* 16 (1966), 81-95;
>
> 4.9 F. M. Cross, Jr., "The History of the Biblical Text in the Light of Discoveries in the Judean Desert," *Harvard Theological Review* 57 (1964), 281-99;
>
> 4.10 S. Jellicoe, *The Septuagint and Modern Study* (Oxford: Clarendon, 1968);
>
> 4.11 P. W. Skehan, "The Biblical Scrolls from Qumran and the Text of the Old Testament," *Biblical Archaeologist* 28 (1965), 87-100;
>
> 4.12 H. B. Swete, *An Introduction to the Old Testament in Greek*; rev. ed., R. R. Ottley; with an appendix containing the letter of Aristeas, ed. H. St. J. Thackeray (Cam-

bridge: University Press, 1914; repr. New York: Ktav, 1968);

4.13 J. W. Wevers, "Septuagint," *Interpreter's Dictionary of the Bible* 4 (ed. G. A. Buttrick; New York and Nashville: Abingdon, 1962), 273-78;

4.14 J. W. Wevers, "Proto-Septuagint Studies," *The Seed of Wisdom: Essays in Honor of T. J. Meek* (ed. W. S. McCullough; Toronto: University of Toronto Press, 1964), 58-77; and

4.15 J. W. Wevers, "Septuaginta Forschungen seit 1954," *Theologische Rundschau* 33 (1968), 18-76.

Chapter Five

# Concordances to the New Testament and Other Relevant Literature

The best concordance available (until the publication of K. Aland, *Vollständige Konkordanz des griechischen Neuen Testaments . . .*) for the New Testament is:

> 5.1    W. F. Moulton and A. S. Geden, *A Concordance to the Greek Testament according to the Texts of Westcott and Hort, Tischendorf and the English Revisers* (Edinburgh: T. & T. Clark, 1897; 3rd ed., 1926; rev. J. Recks, 1963).

Some will find useful the smaller (and incomplete) concordance edited by A. Schmoller:

> 5.2    A. Schmoller, *Handkonkordanz zum griechischen Neuen Testament* (14th ed.; Stuttgart: Württembergische Bibelanstalt, 1968).

Some will also find an English-Greek concordance useful:

> 5.3    G. V. Wigram, *The Englishman's Greek Concordance of the New Testament . . .* (London, 1839; 9th ed., 1903; repr. London: Samuel Bagster & Sons/Grand Rapids: Zondervan).

For the Hebrew text of the Old Testament two good concordances are available:

5.4    S. Mandelkern, *Veteris Testamenti concordantiae Hebraicae atque Chaldaicae* . . . (6th ed.; Jerusalem and Tel-Aviv: Sumptibus Schocken, 1964) and

5.5    G. Lisowsky and L. Rost, *Konkordanz zum hebraischen Alten Testament nach dem von Paul Kahle in der Biblia Hebraica edidit R. Kittel besorgten Masoretischen Text* . . . (2nd ed.; Stuttgart: Württembergische Bibelanstalt, 1958).

Some will also find an English-Hebrew concordance useful:

5.6    G. V. Wigram, *The Englishman's Hebrew and Chaldee Concordance of the Old Testament* . . . (2 vols.; London, 1843; repr. London: Samuel Bagster & Sons/Grand Rapids: Zondervan).

For concordances to English translations (the first two for the Authorized [=King James] Version and the third for the Revised Standard Version) of the whole Bible the following are the most important:

5.7    J. Strong, *The Exhaustive Concordance of the Bible* . . . (New York and Nashville: Abingdon, 1890);

5.8    R. Young, *Analytical Concordance to the Bible* . . . (24th American ed., W. B. Stevenson; New York: Funk & Wagnalls, n.d./ Grand Rapids: Wm. B. Eerdmans); and

5.9    J. W. Ellison, *Nelson's Complete Concordance of the Revised Standard Version Bible* (New York: Thomas Nelson, 1957).

The standard concordance for the Greek Old Testament is:

5.10   E. Hatch and H. Redpath, *A Concordance to
the Septuagint and the Other Greek Versions
of the Old Testament (Including the Apocryphal Books)* (3 vols.; Oxford: Clarendon,
1897-1906; 2-vol. photomechanical repr. at
Graz, Austria: Akademische Druck- u. Ver-
lagsanstalt, 1954).

(On biblical concordances see Danker, ch. 1.)

Concordances to other Hebrew and Greek literature in
antiquity will prove to be useful in New Testament studies. For extrabiblical Jewish literature there are a few
concordances, in addition to that of E. Hatch and H.
Redpath (5.10). For the apocrypha of the Old Testament
the following is available:

5.11   C. A. Wahl, *Clavis librorum Veteris Testamenti apocryphorum philologica* (Lipsiae:
Sumptibus Joannis Ambrosii Barth, 1853).

For the Qumran texts (Dead Sea Scrolls) there is one
concordance and a supplement to it for the major Qumran texts. In addition, some of the publications of specific Qumran texts or collections of them (e.g., *Discoveries
in the Judaean Desert*) include word indices, although
these are not listed here.

5.12   K. G. Kuhn, *Konkordanz zu den Qumrantexten* (Göttingen: Vandenhoeck & Ruprecht, 1960) and

5.13   K. G. Kuhn, "Nachträge zur Konkordanz zu
den Qumrantexten," *Revue de Qumran* 4
(1963), 163-234.

There is no complete concordance for Josephus. The
indices in the Loeb edition of Josephus (12.17) are helpful in the present situation. An unfinished lexicon (ἀ-
ἐμφιλοχωρεῖν) by Thackeray and Marcus is of
some help. The need will be met by the announced
three-volume complete concordance to Josephus (ed. K.
H. Rengstorf; Leiden: E. J. Brill) of which a supplementary volume (covering personal and geographical
names) and Vol. I are already available.

5.14 H. St. J. Thackeray and R. Marcus, *A Lexicon to Josephus* (Publications of the Alexander Kohut Memorial Foundation; Paris: Libraire Orientaliste Paul Geuthner, 1930-55);

5.15 A. Schalit, *Namenwörterbuch zu Flavius Josephus* (A Complete Concordance to Flavius Josephus, Suppl. I; Leiden: E. J. Brill, 1968); and

5.16 K. H. Rengstorf *et al.*, *A Complete Concordance to Flavius Josephus*, Vol. I: A-Δ (Leiden: E. J. Brill, 1972).

There is no easy-to-use nor completely accurate concordance to Philo. The best available is:

5.17 H. Leisegang, printed in the L. Cohn, P. Wendland, S. Reiter text of Philo (Berlin, 1896-1930).

For some early Christian literature convenient concordances are available. There are two concordances to the Apostolic Fathers of which Kraft is the better:

5.18 E. J. Goodspeed, *Index Patristicus sive clavis patrum apostolicorum operum . . .* (Leipzig: J. C. Hinrichs'sche Buchhandlung, 1907) and

5.19 H. Kraft, *Clavis Patrum Apostolicorum* (Darmstadt: Wissenschaftliche Buchgesellschaft, 1964).

Goodspeed also prepared a concordance to the Greek Christian apologetic literature, which has also been conveniently reprinted:

5.20 E. J. Goodspeed, *Index Apologeticus . . .* (Leipzig: J. C. Hinrichs'sche Buchhandlung, 1912) and reprinted almost completely in

5.21 D. Ruiz Bueno, *Padres Apologistas Griegos (s. II) . . .* (Biblioteca de Autores Cristianos 116; Madrid: La Editorial Catolica, 1954), 889-1006.

There will be no attempt here to list concordances to the Greek and Latin literature of classical, Hellenistic and patristic times. There are two guides to concordances for this literature, although both are dated:

5.22 H. and B. Riesenfeld, *Repertorium Lexico-graphicum Graecum: A Catalogue of Indexes and Dictionaries to Greek Authors* (Stockholm: Alquist & Wiksell, 1954) and

5.23 P. Faider, *Répertoire des index et lexiques d'auteurs latins* (Collection d'Études Latines III; Paris: Société d'Édition "Les Belles Lettres," 1926).

The Boston Theological Institute has announced that it will publish a series of Concordances to Patristic and Late Classical Texts, the first of which is:

5.24 D. Georgi and J. Strugnell, *Concordance to the Corpus Hermeticum, Tractate One: The Poimandres* (Concordances to Patristic and Late Classical Texts, Vol. 0, Preliminary Issue; Cambridge: Boston Theological Institute, 1971).

Chapter Six

# Lexicons of the New Testament and Other Relevant Literature

The standard lexicon for the New Testament (and the Apostolic Fathers) is:

6.1   W. Bauer, *A Greek-English Lexicon of the New Testament and Other Early Christian Literature* (trans. W. F. Arndt and F. W. Gingrich from the 4th German ed.; Chicago: University of Chicago Press, 1957).

It should be noted that there is a fifth edition of W. Bauer in German (1958). Another important work for New Testament study is:

6.2   J. H. Moulton and G. Milligan, *The Vocabulary of the Greek Testament Illustrated from the Papyri and Other Non-Literary Sources* (London: Hodder and Stoughton, 1914-30/Grand Rapids: Wm. B. Eerdmans).

Very important is the lexicographic theological dictionary to words and concepts in the New Testament and other relevant literature begun by G. Kittel and continued by G. Friedrich. The work was written in German (*Theologisches Wörterbuch zum Neuen Testament*; abbreviated *TWNT*) and comprises nine volumes. The English translation has been prepared by G. W. Bromiley.

6.3   G. Kittel and G. Friedrich, *Theological Dic-*

*tionary of the New Testament* (trans. G. W. Bromiley; Grand Rapids: Wm. B. Eerdmans, 1964-    ). Vols. I-IV were edited by G. Kittel (1933-42), and Vols. V-IX by G. Friedrich (1954-72). The abbreviation for the English translation is *TDNT.*

Other Greek lexicons are important in New Testament study. For classical (and Hellenistic) Greek literature the standard lexicon is:

    6.4    H. G. Liddell and R. Scott, *A Greek-English Lexicon* (9th ed., H. Stuart Jones and R. McKenzie; Oxford: Clarendon, 1940) and

    6.5    E. A. Barber, P. Maas, M. Scheller and M. L. West, *H. G. Liddell, Robert Scott, H. Stuart Jones, Greek-English Lexicon: A Supplement* (Oxford: Clarendon, 1968).

This lexicon (6.4 and 6.5) is available bound in one volume. For convenience and ease in use there is an abridged form of Liddell-Scott that is useful for rapid reading:

    6.6    *A Lexicon abridged from Liddell and Scott's Greek-English Lexicon* (Oxford: Clarendon, 1871; repr. many times).

For later Hellenistic and Byzantine Greek the following lexicon is important:

    6.7    E. A. Sophocles, *Greek-Lexicon of the Roman and Byzantine Periods (from B. C. 146 to A.D. 1100)* (rev. ed.; 2 vols.; Cambridge, Mass., 1887; repr. New York, 1957).

For Christian patristic literature the following lexicon is very important:

    6.8    G. W. H. Lampe, *A Patristic Greek Lexicon* (Oxford: Clarendon, 1961-68).

There are several lexical aids that can help in the rapid reading of the New Testament (see also 3.2):

6.9 F. W. Gingrich, *Shorter Lexicon of the Greek New Testament* (Chicago: University of Chicago Press, 1965);

6.10 N. E. Han, *A Parsing Guide to the Greek New Testament* (Scottdale: Herald Press, 1971);

6.11 S. Kubo, *A Reader's Greek Lexicon of the New Testament* (Berrien Springs: Andrews University Press, 1971); and

6.12 C. Morrison and D. H. Barnes, *New Testament Word Lists for Rapid Reading of the Greek Testament* (Grand Rapids: Wm. B. Eerdmans, n.d. [1966]).

Three lexical aids are helpful in statistical distribution data regarding words and word-groups:

6.13 X. Jacques, *List of New Testament Words Sharing Common Elements: Supplement to Concordance or Dictionary* (Scripta Pontificii Instituti Biblici 119; Rome: Biblical Institute Press, 1969);

6.14 X. Jacques, *List of Septuagint Words Sharing Common Elements* (Subsidia Biblica 1; Rome: Biblical Institute Press, 1972); and

6.15 R. Morgenthaler, *Statistik des neutestamentlichen Wortschatzes* (Zürich/Frankfort am Main: Gotthelf, 1958).

A good aid in building a New Testament vocabulary is:

6.16 B. M. Metzger, *Lexical Aids for Students of New Testament Greek* (new ed.; published by the author, 1969).

Some will find the following aid helpful in using Bauer's lexicon:

6.17 J. R. Alsop, *Index to the Arndt and Gingrich Greek Lexicon* (2nd ed.; Santa Ana: Wycliffe Bible Translators, 1968)/*An Index to the Bauer-Arndt-Gingrich Greek Lexicon* (Grand Rapids: Zondervan, 1972).

For locating unusual verbal forms in literature outside of the New Testament the following books will be useful:

6.18 N. Marinone and F. Gaula, *Complete Handbook of Greek Verbs* (Cambridge, Mass.: Schoenhof's Books, 1961, 1963) and

6.19 G. Traut, *Lexicon über die Formen der griechischen Verba* (Darmstadt: Wissenschaftliche Buchgesellschaft, 1968 [repr. of the 1867 ed.] ).

For biblical Hebrew these lexicons are significant:

6.20 F. Brown, S. R. Driver and C. A. Briggs, *A Hebrew and English Lexicon of the Old Testament with an Appendix containing the Biblical Aramaic* . . . (Oxford: Clarendon, 1907);

6.21 L. Koehler and W. Baumgartner, *Lexicon in Veteris Testamenti Libros: Wörterbuch zum hebräischen Alten Testament in deutscher und englischer Sprache/A Dictionary of the Hebrew Old Testament in English and German—Wörterbuch zum aramäischen Teil des Alten Testaments in deutscher und englischer Sprache/A Dictionary of the Aramaic Parts of the Old Testament in English and German* (Leiden: E. J. Brill/Grand Rapids: Wm. B. Eerdmans, 1958);

6.22 L. Koehler and W. Baumgartner, *Supplementum ad Lexicon in Veteris Testamenti Libros* (Leiden: E. J. Brill/Grand Rapids: Wm. B. Eerdmans, 1958);

6.23 L. Koehler, W. Baumgartner, B. Hartmann and E. Y. Kutscher, *Hebräisches und Aramäisches Lexikon zum Alten Testament* (3rd ed.; Leiden: E. J. Brill, 1967-  ) [in progress] ; and

6.24  W. L. Holladay, *A Concise Hebrew and Aramaic Lexicon of the Old Testament Based on the First, Second, and Third Editions of the Koehler-Baumgartner Lexicon in Veteris Testamenti Libros* (Leiden: E. J. Brill/Grand Rapids: Wm. B. Eerdmans, 1971)—the most practical Hebrew lexicon.

For rabbinic Hebrew there are three useful lexicons:

6.25  M. Jastrow, *A Dictionary of the Targumim, the Talmud Babli and Yerushalmi, and the Midrashic Literature* (2 vols.; 2nd ed.; New York, 1926; repr. New York: Pardes Publishing House, 1950);

6.26  J. Levy, *Neuhebräisches und chaldäisches Wörterbuch über die Talmudim und Midraschim* (4 vols.; 2nd ed., H. L. Fleischer with L. Goldschmidt; repr. Darmstadt: Wissenschaftliche Buchgesellschaft, 1963); and

6.27  G. H. Dalman, *Aramäisch-neuhebräisches Handwörterbuch zu Targum, Talmud und Midrasch* (3rd ed.; Göttingen, 1938).

(On lexicons see Danker, chs. 6-8.)

# Chapter Seven

# Grammars of the New Testament and Other Relevant Literature

The standard grammar of the New Testament is:

7.1    F. Blass and A. Debrunner, *A Greek Grammar of the New Testament and Other Early Christian Literature* (trans. and rev. of the 9th-10th German ed. incorporating supplementary notes of A. Debrunner by R. W. Funk; Chicago: University of Chicago Press, 1961).

Other grammars and grammatical studies important for the New Testament are:

7.2    J. H. Moulton, *A Grammar of New Testament Greek* (Edinburgh: T. & T. Clark; Vol. I: *Prolegomena*, 3rd ed., 1908; Vol. II: *Accidence and Word-Formation with an Appendix on Semitisms in the New Testament* by J. H. Moulton and W. F. Howard, 1919-29; Vol. III: *Syntax* by N. Turner, 1963)—an excellent, comprehensive resource grammar;

7.3    C. F. D. Moule, *An Idiom Book of New Testament Greek* (2nd ed.; Cambridge: University Press, 1959)—an excellent, selective guide to some particular grammatical problems;

7.4     E. D. Burton, *Syntax of the Moods and Tenses in New Testament Greek* (3rd ed.; Chicago: University of Chicago Press, 1898);

7.5     M. Zerwick, *Biblical Greek Illustrated by Examples* (Eng. ed. adapted from the 4th Latin ed. by J. Smith; Scripta Pontificii Instituti Biblici 114; Rome, 1963)—a very fine intermediate grammar with numerous examples;

7.6     H. E. Dana and J. R. Mantey, *A Manual Grammar of the Greek New Testament* (New York: Macmillan, 1927)—a popular intermediate grammar;

7.7     A. T. Robertson, *A Grammar of the Greek New Testament in the Light of Historical Research* (Nashville: Broadman, 1934)—a massive and classic study; and

7.8     W. Mueller, *Grammatical Aids for Students of New Testament Greek* (Grand Rapids: Wm. B. Eerdmans, 1972).

The standard grammar for classical Greek is:

7.9     H. W. Smyth, *Greek Grammar* (rev. ed., G. M. Messing; Cambridge: Harvard University Press, 1963).

This grammar has no index of passages cited. This need has been filled by:

7.10     W. A. Schumann, *Index of Passages Cited in Herbert Weir Smyth Greek Grammar* (Greek, Roman, and Byzantine Studies Scholarly Aids 1; Cambridge, 1961).

The standard Hebrew grammar for the Old Testament is:

7.11     E. Kautzsch, *Gesenius' Hebrew Grammar* (2nd Eng. ed., A. E. Cowley; Oxford: Clarendon, 1910).

A simpler but very fine Old Testament Hebrew grammar is:

7.12 M. Greenberg, *Introduction to Hebrew* (Englewood Cliffs: Prentice-Hall, 1965).

The standard Hebrew and Aramaic grammars for early rabbinic and biblical Aramaic materials are:

7.13 M. Segal, *A Grammar of Mishnaic Hebrew* (2nd ed.; Oxford: Clarendon, 1958);

7.14 W. B. Stevenson, *Grammar of Palestinian Jewish Aramaic* (2nd ed.; Oxford: Clarendon, 1962); and

7.15 F. Rosenthal, *A Grammar of Biblical Aramaic* (Porta Linguarum Orientalium, Neue Serie V; Wiesbaden: Otto Harrassowitz, 1961).

(On grammars see Danker, chs. 6-8.)

Chapter Eight

# New Testament Introduction, Theology, History and Chronology

Works that deal with the more technical questions of introduction, with the theology of the canon as a whole and with the historical and chronological setting of the New Testament are very useful in the study of New Testament texts.

From the many *introductions* available there are three that are most significant and represent differing points of view:

8.1 D. Guthrie, *New Testament Introduction* (3rd ed.; Downers Grove: Inter-Varsity, 1970);

8.2 W. G. Kümmel, *Introduction to the New Testament* (14th ed.; founded by P. Feine and J. Behm; trans. A. J. Mattill, Jr.; Nashville and New York: Abingdon, 1966)—includes text and canon; and

8.3 A. Wikenhauser, *New Testament Introduction* (trans. J. Cunningham; New York: Herder and Herder, 1958)—includes text and canon.

In addition to these volumes there are other books that deal with introduction in other ways. Two very helpful surveys of the history of New Testament studies are:

8.4　W. G. Kümmel, *The New Testament: The History of the Investigation of Its Problems* (trans. S. M. Gilmour and H. C. Kee; Nashville and New York: Abingdon, 1972) and

8.5　S. Neill, *The Interpretation of the New Testament 1861-1961* (The Firth Lectures, 1962; New York: Oxford University Press, 1964).

A book that approaches introduction with the intent "to investigate the circumstances which led to the making of the New Testament" is:

8.6　C. F. D. Moule, *The Birth of the New Testament* (2nd ed.; Harper's New Testament Commentaries; New York: Harper and Row, 1966).

The one area least accounted for in the introductions noted (8.1-8.3) is the matter of redaction criticism in the study of the synoptic gospels. A survey introduction to this area is:

8.7　J. Rohde, *Rediscovering the Teaching of the Evangelists* (trans. D. M. Barton; The New Testament Library; Philadelphia: Westminster, 1968).

Works in the area of New Testament *theology* abound. From this mass the following seven books should prove to be most helpful:

8.8　R. Bultmann, *Theology of the New Testament* (2 vols.; trans. K. Grobel; New York: Charles Scribner's Sons, 1951, 1955; published also in 1 vol.)—an influential classic that is most helpful on Johannine and Pauline theology;

8.9　H. Conzelmann, *An Outline of the Theology of the New Testament* (trans. J. Bowden; New York: Harper and Row, 1969)—must be understood in conjunction with R. Bultmann's *Theology;*

40

8.10 C. H. Dodd, *The Interpretation of the Fourth Gospel* (Cambridge: University Press, 1953)—a classic presentation of the major themes of the Gospel of John;

8.11 J. Jeremias, [*New Testament Theology;* Vol. I:] *The Proclamation of Jesus* (trans. J. Bowden; New York: Charles Scribner's Sons, 1971)—especially rich on the context of Jesus' teaching within Judaism;

8.12 A. Richardson, *An Introduction to the Theology of the New Testament* (New York: Harper and Brothers, 1958)—helpful for its topical approach;

8.13 R. Schnackenburg, *New Testament Theology Today* (trans. D. Askew; New York: Herder and Herder, 1963)—a survey of trends and issues in New Testament theology; and

8.14 D. E. H. Whiteley, *The Theology of St. Paul* (Philadelphia: Fortress, 1964)—a very fine topical study of a major portion of the New Testament.

For New Testament *history* the following books will provide helpful, general coverage:

8.15 F. F. Bruce, *New Testament History* (Nelson's Library of Theology; London: Thomas Nelson, 1969; Garden City: Doubleday, 1971)—the best of these three;

8.16 F. V. Filson, *A New Testament History: The Story of the Emerging Church* (Westminster Aids to the Study of the Scriptures; Philadelphia: Westminster, 1964); and

8.17 B. Reicke, *The New Testament Era: The World of the Bible from 500 B.C. to A.D. 100* (trans. D. E. Green; Philadelphia: Fortress, 1968). '

*Chronological* problems for the New Testament and its historical environment can be especially difficult. Although not answering all questions, these books will be helpful:

8.18 E. J. Bickerman, *Chronology of the Ancient World* (Aspects of Greek and Roman Life; Ithaca: Cornell University Press, 1968);

8.19 J. Finegan, *Handbook of Biblical Chronology: Principles of Time Reckoning in the Ancient World and Problems of Chronology in the Bible* (Princeton: Princeton University Press, 1964); and

8.20 A. E. Samuel, *Greek and Roman Chronology: Calendars and Years in Classical Antiquity* (Handbuch der Altertumswissenschaft, Erste Abteilung, Siebenter Teil; München: C. H. Beck'sche Verlagsbuchhandlung, 1972).

Chapter Nine

# New Testament Topography, Geography and Archaeology

Bible atlases include materials on both the Old and New Testaments. There are several fine Bible *atlases*:

9.1 Y. Aharoni and M. Avi-Yonah, *The Macmillan Bible Atlas* (New York: Macmillan, 1968)—contains the most useful detail maps with references to the primary sources on which they are based;

9.2 D. Baly and A. D. Tushingham, *Atlas of the Biblical World* (New York: World, 1971);

9.3 L. H. Grollenberg, *Atlas of the Bible* (trans. and ed. J. M. H. Reid and H. H. Rowley; foreword by W. F. Albright and H. H. Rowley; preface by R. de Vaux; London and New York: Thomas Nelson, 1956);

9.4 E. G. Kraeling, *Rand McNally Bible Atlas* (Chicago: Rand McNally, 1956);

9.5 J. H. Negenman, *New Atlas of the Bible* (ed. H. H. Rowley; trans. H. Hoskins and R. Beckley; with a foreword by H. H. Rowley and an epilogue by L. H. Grollenberg; Garden City: Doubleday, 1969); and

9.6 G. E. Wright and F. V. Filson, *The Westminster Historical Atlas to the Bible* (rev. ed.; with an introductory article by W. F. Al-

43

bright; Westminster Aids to the Study of the Scriptures; Philadelphia: Westminster, 1956).

Three other atlases are significant for New Testament study:

9.7   M. Grant and A. Banks, *Ancient History Atlas* (New York: Macmillan, 1971);

9.8   A. A. M. van der Heyden and H. H. Scullard, *Atlas of the Classical World* (London and New York: Thomas Nelson, 1959); and

9.9   F. van der Meer and C. Mohrmann, *Atlas of the Early Christian World* (trans. and ed. M. F. Hedlund and H. H. Rowley; London and New York: Thomas Nelson, 1966).

For biblical *geography* there are the following helpful studies:

9.10   Y. Aharoni, *The Land of the Bible: A Historical Geography* (trans. A. F. Rainey; Philadelphia: Westminster, 1967)—the most helpful of these three;

9.11   M. Avi-Yonah, *The Holy Land from the Persian to the Arab Conquests (536 B.C. to A.D. 640): A Historical Geography* (Grand Rapids: Baker, 1966); and

9.12   D. Baly, *The Geography of the Bible: A Study in Historical Geography* (New York: Harper and Brothers, 1957).

Unfortunately, there is no thorough, scholarly and well-documented book on New Testament *archaeology*. For the present the following will be helpful (see also Danker, ch. 13):

9.13   E. F. Campbell, Jr. and D. N. Freedman, *The Biblical Archaeologist Reader*, Vol. II (Garden City: Doubleday, 1964)—section III deals with "Prominent Cities of the New Testament Period";

9.14 J. Finegan, *The Archaeology of the New Testament: The Life of Jesus and the Beginning of the Early Church* (Princeton: Princeton University Press, 1969)—this contains nothing on the Acts, Paul or Revelation;

9.15 R. K. Harrison, *Archaeology of the New Testament* (Teach Yourself Books; London: The English Universities Press, 1964; repr. London: Hodder and Stoughton, 1967)—a very general survey;

9.16 J. A. Thompson, *Archaeology and the New Testament* (Grand Rapids: Wm. B. Eerdmans, 1960; repr. in J. A. Thompson, *The Bible and Archaeology* [Grand Rapids: Wm. B. Eerdmans, 1962; rev. ed., 1972])—a very general survey; and

9.17 G. E. Wright, *Biblical Archaeology* (rev. ed.; Philadelphia: Westminster, 1962)—chs. XIII and XIV are on New Testament archaeology and are very fine, but brief.

# Chapter Ten

# Dictionaries and Encyclopedias

The many helpful biblical, theological and religious dictionaries and encyclopedias often provide useful and significant data for the study of the New Testament and its historical-religious context.

The best dictionary of the Bible is (see also 6.3):

> 10.1　G. A. Buttrick, *The Interpreter's Dictionary of the Bible* (4 vols.; Nashville and New York: Abingdon, 1962).

A very fine one-volume Bible dictionary is:

> 10.2　J. D. Douglas *et al.*, *The New Bible Dictionary* (Grand Rapids: Wm. B. Eerdmans, 1962).

Two older dictionaries relating to New Testament themes remain helpful:

> 10.3　J. Hastings *et al.*, *A Dictionary of Christ and the Gospels* (2 vols.; Edinburgh: T. & T. Clark/New York: Charles Scribner's Sons, 1906-08) and

> 10.4　J. Hastings *et al.*, *Dictionary of the Apostolic Church* (2 vols.; Edinburgh: T. & T. Clark/New York: Charles Scribner's Sons, 1915-18).

There are three specialized dictionaries that are invaluable in providing relevant data and bibliography on numerous themes and persons of the historical-religious context of the New Testament:

10.5 F. L. Cross, *The Oxford Dictionary of the Christian Church* (New York: Oxford University Press, 1957, 1966);

10.6 N. G. L. Hammond and H. H. Scullard, *The Oxford Classical Dictionary* (2nd ed.; Oxford: Clarendon: 1970); and

10.7 W. Smith and H. Wace, *A Dictionary of Christian Biography, Literature, Sects and Doctrines* (4 vols.; London: John Murray, 1877-87; repr. New York: AMS Press).

Among the large, multi-volume general religious encyclopedias the following are especially helpful (see also the two excellent Jewish encyclopedias, 12.60 and 12.61):

10.8 J. Hastings *et al.*, *Encyclopedia of Religion and Ethics* (13 vols.; Edinburgh: T. & T. Clark/New York: Charles Scribner's Sons, 1908-12);

10.9 *New Catholic Encyclopedia* (15 vols.; New York: McGraw-Hill, 1967)—a superior work;

10.10 S. M. Jackson, *The New Schaff-Herzog Encyclopedia of Religious Knowledge* (13 vols.; New York: Funk and Wagnalls, 1908-12)—which is supplemented by the following item; and

10.11 L. A. Loetscher, *Twentieth Century Encyclopedia of Religious Knowledge* (2 vols.; Grand Rapids: Baker, 1955).

(Danker, ch. 9, discusses dictionaries of the Bible and related subject areas.)

# Chapter Eleven

# Literature, History and Religion of the New Testament World: General and Pagan

## GENERAL

There are three significant bodies of literature that are related to New Testament studies—pagan, Jewish and early Christian (for some data in this area see 8:15 and 8.17). Two excellent general readers for this are:

11.1 E. Barker, *From Alexander to Constantine: Passages and Documents Illustrating the History of Social and Political Ideas 336 B.C.-A.D. 337 Translated with Introductions, Notes, and Essays* (Oxford: Clarendon, 1956) and

11.2 C. K. Barrett, *The New Testament Background: Selected Documents edited with introductions* (London: S.P.C.K., 1956/New York: Harper and Brothers, 1961).

## PAGAN

For a broad, general introduction to classical studies for theological students there is:

11.3 M. R. P. McGuire, *Introduction to Classical Scholarship: A Syllabus and Bibliographical Guide* (rev. ed.; Washington: The Catholic University of American Press, 1961).

The best general reference dictionary for classical studies is the Oxford dictionary noted previously (10.6).

Good surveys of Greek literature are the following (see also previously listed 2.24-2.26, 2.36, 5.22, 6.4-6.5, 6.7, 7.9-7.10, 8.18, 9.8):

11.4　A. Lesky, *A History of Greek Literature* (trans. J. Willis and C. de Heer; New York: Thomas Y. Crowell, 1966) and

11.5　H. J. Rose, *A Handbook of Greek Literature from Homer to the Age of Lucian* (New York: E. P. Dutton, 1960).

Good surveys of Latin literature are the following (see also 2.24-2.26, 2.36, 5.23, 8.18, 9.8):

11.6　J. W. Duff, *A Literary History of Rome from the Origins to the Close of the Golden Age* (ed. A. M. Duff; New York: Barnes and Noble, 1953)—to A.D. 14;

11.7　J. W. Duff, *A Literary History of Rome in the Silver Age from Tiberius to Hadrian* (ed. A. M. Duff; New York: Barnes and Noble, 1960)—A.D. 14-138; and

11.8　H. J. Rose, *A Handbook of Latin Literature from the Earliest Times to the Death of St. Augustine* (New York: E. P. Dutton, 1960).

The most extensive collection of Greek and Latin texts with English translations (approx. 450 vols.) is:

11.9　*The Loeb Classical Library* (Cambridge: Harvard University Press).

For help in finding other English translations of Greek and Latin authors, including some writers not included in the Loeb Classical Library, the following guides are useful:

11.10 F. M. K. Foster, *English Translations from the Greek: A Bibliographical Survey* (Columbia University Studies in English and Comparative Literature; New York: Columbia University Press, 1918);

11.11 A. D. Leeman, *Bibliographia Latina Selecta* (Amsterdam: Adolf M. Hakkert, 1966);

11.12 G. B. Parks and R. Z. Temple, *The Greek and Latin Literatures* (The Literatures of the World in English Translation, A Bibliography, Vol. I, New York: Frederick Ungar, 1968); and

11.13 F. S. Smith, *The Classics in Translation: An Annotated Guide to the Best Translations of the Greek and Latin Classics into English* (New York: Charles Scribner's Sons, 1930).

For surveys of the history of Greece, Rome and the Hellenistic period the following are helpful:

11.14 N. Lewis and M. Reinhold, *Roman Civilization; Sourcebook I: The Republic; Sourcebook II: The Empire* (New York: Columbia University Press, 1955; repr. in paperbacks New York: Harper and Row, 1966);

11.15 M. Rostovtzeff, *Greece* (ed. E. J. Bickerman; trans. J. D. Duff; New York: Oxford University Press, 1963 from the 1930 ed.);

11.16 M. Rostovtzeff, *Rome* (ed. E. J. Bickerman; trans. J. D. Duff; New York: Oxford University Press, 1960 from the 1928 ed.);

11.17 W. W. Tarn, *Hellenistic Civilization* (3rd ed., W. W. Tarn and G. T. Griffith; 1952; Cleveland and New York: World, 1961)—an especially important book; and

11.18 C. B. Welles, *Alexander and the Hellenistic World* (Toronto: Adolf M. Hakkert, 1970).

For more detailed and advanced study in Hellenistic history the following are especially useful:

11.19 S. A. Cook, F. E. Adcock, M. P. Charlesworth and N. H. Baynes, *The Cambridge Ancient History*, Vols. VII-XII (Cambridge: University Press, 1928-39)—this is a magnificent work covering in these volumes from 301 B.C. to A.D. 324;

11.20 M. Rostovtzeff, *The Social and Economic History of the Hellenistic World* (3 vols.; Oxford: Clarendon, 1941); and

11.21 M. Rostovtzeff, *The Social and Economic History of the Roman Empire* (2nd ed., P. M. Fraser; 2 vols.; Oxford: Clarendon, 1957).

Philosophy and religion in the Hellenistic period are treated in the following books:

11.22 A. H. Armstrong, *The Cambridge History of Later Greek and Early Medieval Philosophy* (Cambridge: University Press, 1967);

11.23 A. H. Armstrong, *An Introduction to Ancient Philosophy* (2nd ed., 1949; Boston: Beacon, 1963)—an excellent survey;

11.24 F. Cumont, *The Oriental Religions in Roman Paganism* (1911; New York: Dover, 1956);

11.25 J. Ferguson, *The Religions of the Roman Empire* (Aspects of Greek and Roman Life; Ithaca: Cornell University Press, 1970);

11.26 A. J. Festugière, *Personal Religion Among the Greeks* (Sather Classical Lectures, Vol. 26; Berkeley and Los Angeles: University of California Press, 1954, 1960);

11.27 M. P. Nilsson, *Greek Piety* (trans. H. J. Rose, 1947; New York: W. W. Norton, 1969);

11.28 M. P. Nilsson, *A History of Greek Religion* (2nd ed., 1952; trans. F. J. Fielden; New York: W. W. Norton, 1964); and

11.29 A. D. Nock, *Conversion: The Old and New in Religion from Alexander the Great to Augustine of Hippo* (New York: Oxford University Press, 1933).

Collections of readings in ancient philosophy are numerous and the works of the major philosophers are available in the Loeb Classical Library. One reader for

Hellenistic philosophy (although lacking in middle Platonism) is:

11.30 J. L. Saunders, *Greek and Roman Philosophy after Aristotle* (Readings in the History of Philosophy; New York: Free Press, 1966).

There are two excellent readers for religion in the Hellenistic period:

11.31 F. C. Grant, *Ancient Roman Religion* (The Library of Religion 8; New York: Liberal Arts Press, 1957; repr. Indianapolis: Bobbs-Merrill) and

11.32 F. C. Grant, *Hellenistic Religions: The Age of Syncretism* (The Library of Religion 3; New York: Liberal Arts Press, 1953; repr. Indianapolis: Bobbs-Merrill).

Chapter Twelve

# Literature, History and Religion of the New Testament World: Jewish

The first collection of significant literature in Jewish backgrounds to New Testament studies is the Old Testament (for which see Ch. 4 and appropriate sections of Chs. 5, 6, 7, 9; and see Danker, chs. 12 and 14, for his discussion of Jewish backgrounds to biblical studies).

The remainder of the Jewish literature can be broadly divided into intertestamental and rabbinic. One general reader in Jewish literature is:

12.1 S. W. Baron and J. L. Blau, *Judaism: Post-biblical and Talmudic Period* (The Library of Liberal Arts 135; Indianapolis and New York: Bobbs-Merrill, 1954).

Within the *intertestamental literature* there is the apocryphal and pseudepigraphic literature of which the standard collection is:

12.2 R. H. Charles, *The Apocrypha and Pseudepigrapha of the Old Testament in English with Introductions and Critical and Explanatory Notes to the Several Books* (2 vols.; Oxford: Clarendon, 1913).

This collection does omit several important pseudepigraphic works that are nowhere else in English collected

53

together. These works are: Pseudo-Philo, Biblical Antiquities; Apocalypse of Abraham; Joseph and Asenath; Rest of the Words of Baruch (=Paraleipomena of Jeremiah); Lives of the Prophets; Testament of Abraham; Testament of Isaac; Testament of Jacob; Testament of Job; Pseudo-Phocylides; and Pseudo-Menander (for bibliographies on these and works in R. H. Charles see 2.10).

Helpful guides to this literature are the following (see also 12.24):

12.3 O. Eissfeldt, *The Old Testament: An Introduction . . .* (trans. P. R. Ackroyd; New York: Harper and Row, 1965), pp. 571-637;

12.4 B. M. Metzger, *An Introduction to the Apocrypha* (New York: Oxford University Press, 1957);

12.5 R. H. Pfeiffer, *History of New Testament Times with an Introduction to the Apocrypha* (New York: Harper and Row, 1949)—lengthy coverage of the apocryphal works and good coverage of fragmentary Hellenistic Jewish literature (pp. 197-230 for this fragmentary literature not included in R. H. Charles nor named above; see, however, 2.10); and

12.6 C. C. Torrey, *The Apocryphal Literature: A Brief Introduction* (New Haven: Yale University Press, 1945; repr. Hamden, Conn.: Archon Books, 1963).

The lack of modern and available English translations of pseudepigraphic literature not included in Charles (12.2) has begun to be supplied by a series sponsored by the Society of Biblical Literature Pseudepigrapha Seminar. The first two volumes in this series are (Greek text and Eng. trans.):

12.7 R. A. Kraft and A.-E. Purintun, *Paraleipomena Jeremiou* (Texts and Translations 1, Pseudepigrapha Series 1; Society of Biblical Literature, 1972) and

12.8 M. E. Stone, *The Testament of Abraham: The Greek Recensions* (Texts and Translations 2, Pseudepigrapha Series 2; Society of Biblical Literature, 1972).

The Greek texts of the fragmentary Hellenistic/Jewish literature have been collected:

12.9 A.-M. Denis, *Fragmenta pseudepigraphorum quae supersunt Graeca una cum historicorum et auctorum Judaeorum hellenistarum fragmentis collegit et ordinavit* (Pseudepigrapha Veteris Testamenti Graece, Volumen Tertium; Leiden: E. J. Brill, 1970; bound with M. Black, *Apocalypsis Henochi Graece*).

Another important area of intertestamental Jewish literature is that from Qumran known as the Dead Sea Scrolls (for concordances see 5.12 and 5.13; for bibliographies see 2.11-2.15). A listing of published texts of the Dead Sea Scrolls (which needs updating) is:

12.10 J. A. Sanders, "Palestinian Manuscripts 1947-1967," *Journal of Biblical Literature* 86 (1967), 431-40.

There is a convenient edition of the Hebrew text of the major Dead Sea Scrolls (with German trans.):

12.11 E. Lohse, *Die Texte aus Qumran: Hebräisch und deutsch mit masoretischer Punktation, Übersetzung, Einführung und Anmerkungen* (München: Kösel-Verlag/Darmstadt: Wissenschaftliche Buchgesellschaft, 1964).

There are several collections of English translations of the major Dead Sea Scroll texts the most helpful of which are Dupont-Sommer (12.13) and Vermes (12.15):

12.12 M. Burrows, *The Dead Sea Scrolls* (New York: Viking, 1955; paperback ed., 1968), pp. 347-415 and *More Light on the Dead Sea Scrolls: New Scrolls and New Interpreta-*

*tions with Translations of Important Recent Discoveries* (New York: Viking, 1958), pp. 385-404;

12.13 A. Dupont-Sommer, *The Essene Writings from Qumran* (trans. G. Vermes; Cleveland and New York: World, 1961);

12.14 T. H. Gaster, *The Dead Sea Scriptures in English Translation with Introduction and Notes* (rev. ed.; Garden City: Doubleday, 1964); and

12.15 G. Vermes, *The Dead Sea Scrolls in English* (Baltimore: Penguin, 1962, 1965).

Finally, within the broad scope of intertestamental literature are the important figures Philo and Josephus (for concordances and bibliographies on them see 2.10, 2.16-2.18 and 5.14-5.17). The best English translations of Philo and Josephus, which also include a Greek text, are:

12.16 F. H. Colson, G. H. Whitaker and R. Marcus, *Philo* (12 vols.; Loeb Classical Library; Cambridge: Harvard University Press, 1929-53) and

12.17 H. St. J. Thackeray, R. Marcus, A. Wikgren and L. H. Feldman, *Josephus* (9 vols.; Loeb Classical Library; Cambridge: Harvard University Press, 1926-65).

Some will appreciate the few available inexpensive paperback English translations of portions of Philo and Josephus:

12.18 N. N. Glatzer, *Philo Judaeus, The Essential Philo* (New York: Schocken Books, 1971)—basically a reprint of the C. D. Yonge 1854 translation of some of Philo's key writings;

12.19 N. N. Glatzer, *Flavius Josephus, The Second Jewish Commonwealth from the Maccabaean Rebellion to the Outbreak of the Judaeo-Roman War* (New York: Schocken Books, 1971)—basically a reprint of the W.

Whiston-A. R. Shilleto 1889 translation of *Jewish Antiquities* 12.154-20.268; and

12.20 G. A. Williamson, *Josephus, The Jewish War Translated with an Introduction* (rev. ed.; Baltimore: Penguin, 1970).

The history and religion of Judaism in the intertestamental period is covered in the following volumes (see also 12.5):

12.21 F. M. Cross, Jr., *The Ancient Library of Qumran and Modern Biblical Studies* (2nd ed.; Garden City: Doubleday, 1961);

12.22 D. S. Russell, *The Jews from Alexander to Herod* (The New Clarendon Bible, Old Testament, Vol. V; New York: Oxford University Press, 1967);

12.23 D. S. Russell, *The Method & Message of Jewish Apocalyptic 200 BC-AD 100* (The Old Testament Library; Philadelphia: Westminster, 1964); and

12.24 E. Schürer, *A History of the Jewish People in the Times of Jesus Christ* (2nd ed.; 5 vols.; trans. J. Macpherson, S. Taylor and P. Christie; New York: Charles Scribner's Sons, 1886-90); a revised and abridged edition of the first two volumes edited by N. N. Glatzer, *A History of the Jewish People in the Time of Jesus* (New York: Schocken Books, 1961) and a revised edition of the fifth volume edited by N. N. Glatzer, *The Literature of the Jewish People in the Time of Jesus* (New York: Schocken Books, 1972), have appeared.

The *rabbinic literature* of Judaism is extensive and much of it is not available in English translations (for lexicons and grammars see 6.25-6.27 and 7.13-7.14). One good comprehensive anthology is:

12.25 C. G. Montefiore and H. Loewe, *A Rabbinic*

*Anthology selected and arranged with com-
ments and introductions* (London: Macmillan, 1938; repr. Cleveland and New York:
World, and Philadelphia: Jewish Publication
Society of America, 1960).

Targumic literature is a field in flux especially because
of the discovery of Codex Neofiti I (an edition of a
Jerusalem Targum), which is not yet fully published (for
a bibliography to targumic studies see 2.19). The most
extensive English translation of the targums is:

12.26 J. W. Etheridge, *The Targums of Onkelos
and Jonathan Ben Uzziel on the Pentateuch
with the Fragments of the Jerusalem Targum
from the Chaldee* (2 vols.; London, 1862-65;
repr. New York: Ktav, 1968).

Some of the Codex Neofiti I has been published in an
edition that includes an English translation (by M. McNamara and M. Maher):

12.27 A. Díez Macho, *Neophyti 1: Targum Pales-
tinense MS de la Biblioteca Vaticana;* Tomo
I: *Génesis* . . . (Textos y Estudios 7; Madrid:
Consejo Superior de Investigaciones Científi-
cas, 1968) and

12.28 A. Díez Macho, *Neophyti 1: Targum Pales-
tinense MS de la Biblioteca Vaticana;* Tomo
II: *Éxodo* . . . (Textos y Estudios 8; Madrid:
Consejo Superior de Investigaciones Científi-
cas, 1970).

For further reading and details on the targumic literature
the following books are especially helpful:

12.29 J. Bowker, *The Targums and Rabbinic Literature: An Introduction to Jewish Interpretations of Scripture* (Cambridge: University
Press, 1969);

12.30 M. McNamara, *The New Testament and the
Palestinian Targum to the Pentateuch* (Ana-

lecta Biblica 27; Rome: Pontifical Biblical
Institute, 1966); and

12.31 M. McNamara, *Targum and Testament; Aramaic Paraphrases of the Hebrew Bible: A Light on the New Testament* (Shannon: Irish University Press/Grand Rapids: Wm. B. Eerdmans, 1972).

An excellent and most convenient English translation of the Mishnah is:

12.32 H. Danby, *The Mishnah translated from the Hebrew with Introduction and Brief Explanatory Notes* (Oxford: University Press, 1933).

An edition of the Hebrew text with English translation is:

12.33 P. Blackman, *Mishnayoth* (3rd ed.; 7 vols.; New York: Judaica, 1965).

Although there is no complete English translation of the Tosephta, three of the tractates are available in English translations:

12.34 H. Danby, *Tractate Sanhedrin: Mishna and Tosefta* (Translations of Early Documents, Series III: Rabbinic Texts; London: S.P.C.K., 1919);

12.35 A. W. Greenup, *Tractate Sukkah: Mishna and Tosephta* (Translations of Early Documents, Series III: Rabbinic Texts; London: S.P.C.K., 1925); and

12.36 A. L. Williams, *Tractate Berakoth: Mishna and Tosephta* (Translations of Early Documents, Series III: Rabbinic Texts; London: S.P.C.K., 1921).

The Babylonian Talmud has appeared in a good English translation:

12.37 I. Epstein, *The Babylonian Talmud* (35 vols.; London: Soncino, 1935-52; 18-vol. ed., 1961).

There is an English translation of the extracanonical tractates that follow the tractates of the fourth order in most editions of the Babylonian Talmud:

12.38 A. Cohen, *The Minor Tractates of the Talmud: Massektoth Ḳeṭannoth* (2 vols.; London: Soncino, 1965).

There is no English translation of the complete Jerusalem (or Palestinian) Talmud.

A limited amount of the midrashic literature is available in English translation. One of the Tannaitic midrashim, the Mekilta on Exodus, is available in a complete English translation:

12.39 J. Z. Lauterbach, *Mekilta de-Rabbi Ishmael: A Critical Edition on the Basis of the Manuscripts and Early Editions with an English Translation, Introduction and Notes* (3 vols.; The Schiff Library of Jewish Classics; Philadelphia: Jewish Publication Society of America, 1933-35).

There is an English translation of selections from the Tannaitic Sifre on Numbers:

12.40 P. P. Levertoff, *Midrash Sifre on Numbers: Selections from Early Rabbinic Scriptural Interpretations translated from the Hebrew, with brief annotations, and with special reference to the New Testament* (with an introduction by G. H. Box; Translations of Early Documents, Series III: Rabbinic Texts; London: S.P.C.K., 1926).

The most extensive collection of midrashim, from the Amoraic period and even later, that is available in English translation is the Midrash Rabbah:

12.41 H. Freedman and M. Simon, *Midrash Rabbah translated into English with notes, glossary and indices* (10 vols.; London: Soncino, 1939).

Two other midrashim (*ca.* ninth century) are available in English translations:

12.42 W. G. Braude, *The Midrash on Psalms* (2 vols.; Yale Judaica Series 13; New Haven: Yale University Press, 1959) and

12.43 W. G. Braude, *Pesikta Rabbati: Discourses for Feasts, Fasts, and Special Sabbaths Translated* (2 vols.; Yale Judaica Series 18; New Haven: Yale University Press, 1969).

Two other rabbinic works, one from the first century and the second from the ninth century in its present form, are available in English translations:

12.44 S. Zeitlin, *Megillat Taanit as a Source for Jewish Chronology and History in the Hellenistic and Roman Periods* (Philadelphia, 1922; also printed in the *Jewish Quarterly Review* 9 [1918/19], 71-102; 10 [1919/20], 49-80, 237-90 and the translation alone in his *The Rise and Fall of the Judean State;* Vol. II: *37 B.C.E.-66 C.E.* [Philadelphia: Jewish Publication Society of America, 1967], pp. 363-65 [also in 12.55, Vol. 2, pp. 698-700]) and

12.45 G. Friedländer, *Pirke de Rabbi Eliezer (The Chapters of Rabbi Eliezer the Great) according to the Text of the Manuscript belonging to Abraham Epstein of Vienna translated and annotated with introduction and indices* (New York: Bloch, 1916; repr. New York: Hermon Press, 1965, 1970).

Helpful guides to the rabbinic literature are available. One of the best is ch. 4 (pp. 40-92) of J. Bowker's book (see 12.29). Two other useful works are:

12.46 W. O. E. Oesterley and G. H. Box, *A Short Survey of the Literature of Rabbinical and Mediaeval Judaism* (London: S.P.C.K., 1920) and

12.47 H. L. Strack, *Introduction to the Talmud and Midrash* (Philadelphia: The Jewish Publication Society of America, 1931; repr. Cleveland and New York: World/Philadelphia: Jewish Publication Society of America, 1959 and New York: Atheneum, 1969).

Rabbinic theology is well summarized with extensive references to the Talmud in the following books:

12.48 G. F. Moore, *Judaism in the First Three Centuries of the Christian Era: The Age of the Tannaim* (3 vols.; Cambridge: Harvard University Press, 1927-30/the two vols. of text repr. New York: Schocken Books, 1971);

12.49 S. Schechter, *Aspects of Rabbinic Theology* (New York: Macmillan, 1909; repr. New York: Schocken Books, 1961); and

12.50 R. A. Stewart, *Rabbinic Theology: An Introductory Study* (Edinburgh and London: Oliver and Boyd, 1961).

For the history of the rabbinic period the following books will be helpful:

12.51 J. Goldin, "The Period of the Talmud (135 B.C.E.-1035 C.E.)," *The Jews: Their History, Culture, and Religion* (3rd ed., L. Finkelstein; New York: Harper and Brothers, 1960; repr. New York: Schocken Books, 4th ed., 1970), pp. 115-215;

12.52 A. Guttmann, *Rabbinic Judaism in the Making: A Chapter in the History of the Halakhah from Ezra to Judah I* (Detroit: Wayne State University Press, 1970);

12.53 J. Neusner, *A History of Jews in Babylonia* (5 vols.; Studia Post-Biblica IX, XI, XII, XIV, XV; Leiden: E. J. Brill, 1965-70; Vol. 1, 2nd ed., 1969); and

12.54 J. Neusner, *There We Sat Down: Talmudic Judaism in the Making* (Nashville and New York: Abingdon, 1972).

The most extensive collection of rabbinic parallels to the New Testament, H. L. Strack and P. Billerbeck's *Kommentar zum Neuen Testament aus Talmud und Midrasch*, is not available in English. Until publication of the *Compendia Rerum Iudaicarum ad Novum Testamentum*, the following three books cover the gospel material and setting:

12.55 A. Edersheim, *The Life and Times of Jesus the Messiah* (3rd ed.; 2 vols.; New York: Longmans, Green, 1886; repr. Grand Rapids: Wm. B. Eerdmans, 1947/1-vol. ed., 1972);

12.56 J. Jeremias, *Jerusalem in the Time of Jesus: An Investigation into Economic and Social Conditions during the New Testament Period* (trans. F. H. and C. H. Cave; Philadelphia: Fortress, 1969); and

12.57 C. G. Montefiore, *Rabbinic Literature and Gospel Teachings* (London: Macmillan, 1930; repr. New York: Ktav, 1970).

An excellent thematic collection of data from rabbinic (and other Jewish) sources is:

12.58 L. Ginzberg, *The Legends of the Jews* (7 vols.; trans. H. Szold and P. Radin; index by B. Cohen; Philadelphia: Jewish Publication Society of America, 1909-38).

Finally, there are three very significant multi-volume reference works for studies in Judaism in general:

12.59 E. R. Goodenough, *Jewish Symbols in the Greco-Roman Period* (13 vols.; Bollingen Series XXXVII; New York: Pantheon Books, 1953-68);

12.60 I. Singer, *The Jewish Encyclopedia . . .* (12 vols.; New York: Funk and Wagnalls, 1901-06; repr. New York: Ktav); and

12.61 *Encyclopaedia Judaica* (16 vols.; Jerusalem: Encyclopaedia Judaica/New York: Macmillan, 1971-72).

# Chapter Thirteen

# Literature, History and Religion of the New Testament World: Early Christian

The New Testament is part of the literary production of the early Christian church. It is very helpful for understanding the development of the Christian faith and church to have an acquaintance with other literature of the early church (to *ca.* A.D. 250) (see also 2.2, 2.27-2.32, 2.35-2.36, 5.18-5.21, 6.8, 7.1, 9.9, 10.5, 10.7-10.11).

There are several general readers or source books of early Christian literature. The most helpful is:

> 13.1 J. Stevenson, *A New Eusebius: Documents Illustrative of the History of the Church to A.D. 337* (London: S.P.C.K., 1957).

Other useful collections of extracts from early Christian literature are:

> 13.2 H. Bettenson, *The Early Christian Fathers: A Selection from the Writings of the Fathers from St. Clement of Rome to St. Athanasius* (New York: Oxford University Press, 1956);

> 13.3 A. Fremantle, *A Treasury of Early Christianity* (New York: The New American Library, 1953);

> 13.4 W. A. Jurgens, *The Faith of the Early Fathers: A Source-Book of Theological and Historical Passages from the Christian Writ-*

*ings of the Pre-Nicene and Nicene Eras se-
lected and translated* (Collegeville: Liturgical
Press, 1970);

13.5 H. Musurillo, *The Fathers of the Primitive
Church* (New York: New American Library,
1966); and

13.6 D. J. Theron, *Evidence of Tradition: Selected Source Material for the Study of the
History of the Early Church, the New Testament Books, the New Testament Canon*
(Grand Rapids: Baker, 1957).

Better than reading from handbooks is to read complete works from early Christian literature. There are
certain convenient and significant groupings of certain
works. For the Apostolic Fathers there is a Greek text
with facing English translation:

13.7 K. Lake, *The Apostolic Fathers with an English Translation* (2 vols.; The Loeb Classical
Library 24, 25; Cambridge: Harvard University Press, 1912-13).

For the Apostolic Fathers there is a set of commentaries:

13.8 R. M. Grant, *The Apostolic Fathers: A New
Translation and Commentary* (6 vols.; Camden: Thomas Nelson, 1964-68):

Vol. I:   *An Introduction* (R. M. Grant, 1964);
Vol. II:  *First and Second Clement* (R. M. Grant and
          H. H. Graham, 1965);
Vol. III: *Barnabas and the Didache* (R. A. Kraft,
          1965);
Vol. IV:  *Ignatius of Antioch* (R. M. Grant, 1966);
Vol. V:   *Polycarp, Martyrdom of Polycarp, Frag-
          ments of Papias* (W. R. Schoedel, 1967); and
Vol. VI:  *The Shepherd of Hermas* (G. F. Snyder,
          1968).

For the earliest extant Christian historian, Eusebius,
there is also a Greek text with facing English translation:

13.9 K. Lake, J. E. L. Oulton and H. J. Lawlor,
*Eusebius, The Ecclesiastical History with an
English Translation* (2 vols.; The Loeb Classi-

cal Library 153, 265; Cambridge: Harvard University Press, 1926, 1932).

There is an English translation with extensive notes on Eusebius' *Ecclesiastical History* that serves as a commentary:

13.10 H. J. Lawlor and J. E. L. Oulton, *Eusebius, Bishop of Caesarea, The Ecclesiastical History and the Martyrs of Palestine translated with Introduction and Notes* (2 vols.; London: S.P.C.K., 1927-28).

For the apocryphal New Testament there are two major collections of material in English translation:

13.11 E. Hennecke, *New Testament Apocrypha* (2 vols.; ed. W. Schneemelcher; Eng. trans. and ed. R. McL. Wilson; Philadelphia: Westminster, 1963, 1965)—this is the better edition with excellent introductions and bibliographies; and

13.12 M. R. James, *The Apocryphal New Testament being the Apocryphal Gospels, Acts, Epistles, and Apocalypses with Other Narratives and Fragments newly translated* (Oxford: Clarendon, 1924; repr. 1953 with appendixes by J. W. B. Barns).

Apocryphal gospel materials, including texts, are found in the following:

13.13 J. Finegan, *Hidden Records of the Life of Jesus. . .* (Philadelphia/Boston: Pilgrim Press, 1969)—this contains English translations; and

13.14 A. de Santos Otero, *Los Evangelios Apocrifos: Colección de textos griegos y latinos, versión crítica, estudios introductorios, comentarios e ilustraciones* (Biblioteca de Autores Cristianos 148; Madrid: La Editorial Catolica, 1963)—this is the more complete and excellent edition.

An edition of the apocryphal acts is available:

13.15 R. A. Lipsius and M. Bonnet, *Acta Apostolorum Apocrypha* (2 vols. in 3; Lipsiae: In aedibus Hermanni Mendelssohn, 1891-1903; repr. Darmstadt: Wissenschaftliche Buchgesellschaft, 1959).

A fine edition of the Greek apologists is available:

13.16 D. Ruiz Bueno, *Padres Apologistas Griegos (s. II): Introducciones, texto griego, versión española y notas* (Biblioteca de Autores Cristianos 116; Madrid: La Editorial Catolica, 1954).

A superb edition of the Greek and Latin texts with English translations of the martyr acts is available:

13.17 H. Musurillo, *The Acts of the Christian Martyrs: Introduction, Texts and Translations* (Oxford Early Christian Texts; Oxford: Clarendon, 1972).

There is as yet no convenient collection of the Nag Hammadi gnostic texts (for details on what translations are available see 2.29). There are two good English readers on gnosticism that include some Nag Hammadi texts as well as patristic materials:

13.18 R. M. Grant, *Gnosticism: A Source Book of Heretical Writings from the Early Christian Period* (New York: Harper and Brothers, 1961) and

13.19 R. Haardt, *Gnosis: Character and Testimony* (trans. J. F. Hendry; Leiden: E. J. Brill, 1971).

A convenient reader of Greek and Latin patristic texts on gnosticism is:

13.20 W. Völker, *Quellen zur Geschichte der christlichen Gnosis* (Sammlung ausgewählter kirchen- und dogmengeschichtlicher Quellen-schriften, Neue Folge 5; Tübingen: J. C. B. Mohr, 1932).

For extensive collections of early Christian literature certain series provide the majority of the texts most conveniently (for special editions and translations of early Christian works consult 2.27, 2.35 and 13.31-13.34). The major series of English translations of patristic texts are:

13.21 *Ancient Christian Writers: The Works of the Fathers in Translation* (ed. J. Quasten and J. C. Plumpe; Westminster: Newman, 1946-continuing; many vols.);

13.22 *The Ante-Nicene Fathers: Translations of the Writings of the Fathers down to A.D. 325* (10 vols.; ed. A. Roberts, J. Donaldson, A. C. Coxe and A. Menzies; Buffalo, 1884-86; repr. Grand Rapids: Wm. B. Eerdmans);

13.23 *The Fathers of the Church: A New Translation* (currently Washington: Catholic University of America Press, 1947-continuing; many vols.);

13.24 *The Library of Christian Classics* (ed. J. Baillie, J. T. McNeill and H. P. Van Dusen; Philadelphia: Westminster, Vols. I [1953; repr. New York: Macmillan, 1970], II [1954] and V [1956]); and

13.25 *Oxford Early Christian Texts* (ed. H. Chadwick; Oxford: University Press, 1970-continuing)—contains Greek or Latin text, too (see 13.17).

The most important collection of Greek patristic texts is:

13.26 *Die griechischen christlichen Schriftsteller der ersten drei Jahrhunderte* (Berlin, 1897-continuing; many vols.)—abbreviated GCS.

The two most important collections of Latin patristic texts are:

13.27 *Corpus Scriptorum Ecclesiasticorum Latinorum* (Vienna, 1866-continuing; many vols.) —abbreviated CSEL; and

13.28 *Corpus Christianorum, Series Latina* (Turnhout: Brepols, 1954-continuing; many vols.) —abbreviated CCSL.

A very important and extensive (over 160 vols. by 1970) series containing both Greek and Latin patristic texts (with French trans.) is:

13.29 *Sources Chrétiennes* (Paris: Les Éditions du Cerf, 1941-continuing; many vols.)—abbreviated SC.

The most complete collection of patristic texts, which needs to be consulted when no critical text is available, exists in two series:

13.30 *Patrologiae cursus completus, series latina* (ed. J.-P. Migne; Paris, 1844-55; 221 vols.)— abbreviated PL, ML or MPL; and

13.31 *Patrologiae cursus completus, series graeca* (ed. J.-P. Migne; Paris, 1857-66; 161 vols.)— abbreviated PG, MG or MPG.

The most important handbooks or guides to early Christian literature are:

13.32 B. Altaner, *Patrology* (trans. H. C. Graef; New York: Herder and Herder, 1961) and

13.33 J. Quasten, *Patrology* (3 vols.; Westminster: Newman, 1950-60).

Also very useful is the brief book:

13.34 E. J. Goodspeed, *A History of Early Christian Literature* (rev. and enl. by R. M. Grant; Chicago: University of Chicago Press, 1966).

The history of the early church is well covered in the following studies:

13.35 H. Chadwick, *The Early Church* (The Pelican

History of the Church 1; Baltimore: Penguin, 1967/Grand Rapids: Wm. B. Eerdmans, 1968);

13.36 J. G. Davies, *The Early Christian Church* (Garden City: Doubleday, 1965);

13.37 W. H. C. Frend, *The Early Church* (Knowing Christianity; Philadelphia and New York: J. B. Lippincott, 1965);

13.38 R. M. Grant, *Augustus to Constantine: The Thrust of the Christian Movement into the Roman World* (New York: Harper and Row, 1970); and

13.39 H. Lietzmann, *A History of the Early Church* (trans. B. L. Woolf; 4 vols.; 1937-51; repr. in 2 vols. Cleveland and New York: World, 1961).

The theological developments in early Christianity are summarized in these two volumes:

13.40 J. N. D. Kelly, *Early Christian Creeds* (2nd ed.; New York: David MacKay, 1960) and

13.41 J. N. D. Kelly, *Early Christian Doctrines* (2nd ed.; New York: Harper and Brothers, 1960; 4th ed.; London: Adam and Charles Black, 1968).

# Chapter Fourteen

# English Translations of the New Testament

Exegetical study of the New Testament can be enriched by the knowledge and use of English translations of the text. A brief illustration of this may be seen in Danker's discussion of "the use of English Bible versions" (chs. 10 and 11).

The best one-volume history of the English translations of the Bible is:

14.1 F. F. Bruce, *The English Bible: A History of Translations from the earliest English Versions to the New English Bible* (rev. ed.; New York: Oxford University Press, 1970).

Other volumes that will be helpful in the history of English translations of the Bible are:

14.2 P. R. Ackroyd and C. F. Evans, *The Cambridge History of the Bible;* Vol. 1: *From the Beginnings to Jerome* (Cambridge: University Press, 1970);

14.3 S. L. Greenslade, *The Cambridge History of the Bible;* [Vol. 3:] *The West from the Reformation to the Present Day* (Cambridge: University Press, 1963);

14.4 G. W. H. Lampe, *The Cambridge History of the Bible;* Vol. 2: *The West from the Fathers to the Reformation* (Cambridge: University Press, 1969);

14.5  G. MacGregor, *A Literary History of the Bible: From the Middle Ages to the Present Day* (Nashville and New York: Abingdon, 1968);

14.6  A. W. Pollard, *Records of the English Bible: The Documents Relating to the Translation and Publication of the Bible in English, 1525-1611* (London: Henry Frowde/Oxford University Press, 1911); and

14.7  E. H. Robertson, *The New Translations of the Bible* (Studies in Ministry and Worship 12; London: SCM/Naperville: Alec R. Allenson, 1959)—concentrates on the twentieth century.

For specific data on various translations and editions the following catalogs will be useful:

14.8  A. S. Herbert, *Historical Catalogue of Printed Editions of the English Bible 1525-1961* (rev. and enl. from the ed. of T. H. Darlow and H. F. Moule, 1903; London: British and Foreign Bible Society/New York: American Bible Society, 1968);

14.9  M. T. Hills, *The English Bible in America: A Bibliography of Editions of the Bible & New Testament Published in America 1777-1957* (New York: American Bible Society and The New York Public Library, 1961); and

14.10 E. B. O'Callaghan, *A List of Editions of the Holy Scriptures and Parts thereof printed in America previous to 1860 with introduction and bibliographical notes* (Albany: Munsell & Rowland, 1861; repr. Detroit: Gale Research Company, Book Tower, 1966).

There have been over sixty English translations of the New Testament (or significant parts thereof) published in the twentieth century. Many of them are worthy of consultation by the New Testament exegete, but a few that may be most suggestive for exegesis are recommended here (with original publishers and dates of first complete editions):

14.11 W. Barclay, *The New Testament: A New Translation* (2 vols.; London: Collins, 1968-69);

14.12 W. F. Beck, *The New Testament in the Language of Today* (St. Louis: Concordia, 1963, 1967);

14.13 R. G. Bratcher, *Good News for Modern Man: The New Testament in Today's English Version* (New York: American Bible Society, 1966; 3rd ed., 1971);

14.14 F. F. Bruce, *The Letters of Paul: An Expanded Paraphrase* . . . (Grand Rapids: Wm. B. Eerdmans, 1965);

14.15 *The New American Bible: The New Testament* (Paterson: St. Anthony Guild Press, 1970);

14.16 *The New English Bible: New Testament* (Oxford: University Press/Cambridge: University Press, 1961; rev. ed., 1970); and

14.17 J. B. Phillips, *The New Testament in Modern English* (London: Geoffrey Bles, 1958).

Chapter Fifteen

# Commentaries on the New Testament

The commentaries noted here are those that deal with the New Testament text in terms of the historical, cultural, religious and linguistic perspectives of the first century A.D. Homiletic and devotional commentaries have been excluded.

An attempt is made here to reflect a broadly based critical judgment about which commentaries are best. No particular series has been selected for emphasis, simply because the best commentaries are not restricted to any one author or any one series. There are at least two but no more than five commentaries listed in alphabetical order for each of the New Testament books. All of those listed are generally very good English commentaries, often representing various theological and critical positions; in a few cases brief annotations note especially outstanding volumes. Commentaries on New Testament books published in a volume(s) containing several commentaries (e.g., *The Interpreter's Bible*) are not included.

(Consult Danker, ch. 15, for his list of commentaries, which does include significant French and German works.)

Before listing commentaries for individual books, a very few good one-volume commentaries, representing varying viewpoints, are noted:

15.1 M. Black and H. H. Rowley, *Peake's Commentary on the Bible* (Camden: Thomas Nelson, 1962)—probably the most exegetically suggestive of this group;

15.2 R. E. Brown, J. A. Fitzmyer and R. E. Murphy, *The Jerome Biblical Commentary* (Englewood Cliffs: Prentice-Hall, 1968);

15.3 D. Guthrie, J. A. Motyer, A. M. Stibbs and D. J. Wiseman, *The New Bible Commentary: Revised* (Grand Rapids: Wm. B. Eerdmans, 1970); and

15.4 C. M. Laymon, *The Interpreter's One-Volume Commentary on the Bible including the Apocrypha with General Articles* (Nashville and New York: Abingdon, 1971).

(The following abbreviations are used—HNTC: Harper's New Testament Commentaries; ICC: International Critical Commentary; MNTC: Moffatt New Testament Commentary; NIC: New International Commentary; TNTC: Tyndale New Testament Commentaries.)

## Matthew

15.5 W. C. Allen, *A Critical and Exegetical Commentary on the Gospel according to S. Matthew* (3rd ed.; ICC; Edinburgh: T. & T. Clark, 1912);

15.6 D. Hill, *The Gospel of Matthew* (New Century Bible; London: Oliphants, 1972);

15.7 A. H. McNeile, *The Gospel According to St. Matthew: The Greek Text with Introduction, Notes and Indices* (London: Macmillan, 1915)—the best on this gospel; and

15.8 A. Plummer, *An Exegetical Commentary on the Gospel According to S. Matthew* (2nd ed.; London: Elliot Stock, 1910; repr. Grand Rapids: Wm. B. Eerdmans, 1953).

## Mark

15.9 C. E. B. Cranfield, *The Gospel According to Saint Mark: An Introduction and Commentary* (Cambridge Greek Testament Commentary; Cambridge: University Press, 1959)

—with Taylor (15.12) the best combination on this gospel;

15.10 D. E. Nineham, *The Gospel of St. Mark* (The Pelican Gospel Commentaries; Baltimore: Penguin, 1964);

15.11 E. Schweizer, *The Good News according to Mark* (trans. D. H. Madvig; Richmond: John Knox, 1970); and

15.12 V. Taylor, *The Gospel according to St. Mark: The Greek Text with Introduction, Notes, and Indexes* (2nd ed.; London: Macmillan/New York: St. Martin's, 1966)—(see 15.9).

### Luke

15.13 W. F. Arndt, *The Gospel According to St. Luke* (Bible Commentary; St. Louis: Concordia, 1956);

15.14 G. B. Caird, *The Gospel of St. Luke* (The Pelican Gospel Commentaries; Baltimore: Penguin, 1963);

15.15 J. M. Creed, *The Gospel according to St. Luke: The Greek Text with Introduction, Notes, and Indices* (London: Macmillan, 1930);

15.16 E. E. Ellis, *The Gospel of Luke* (The Century Bible, New Ed.; London: Thomas Nelson, 1966); and

15.17 A. Plummer, *A Critical and Exegetical Commentary on the Gospel According to St. Luke* (10th ed.; ICC; Edinburgh: T. & T. Clark, 1914).

### John

15.18 C. K. Barrett, *The Gospel According to St John: An Introduction with Commentary and Notes on the Greek Text* (London: S.P.C.K., 1955, 1958);

15.19 R. E. Brown, *The Gospel According to John (i-xii): Introduction, Translation, and Notes* (The Anchor Bible 29; Garden City: Doubleday, 1966) and *The Gospel According to John (xiii-xxi): Introduction, Translation, and Notes* (The Anchor Bible 29A; Garden City: Doubleday, 1970)—a superior commentary;

15.20 R. Bultmann, *The Gospel of John: A Commentary* (trans. G. R. Beasley-Murray, R. W. N. Hoare and J. K. Riches; Philadelphia: Westminster, 1971);

15.21 L. Morris, *Commentary on the Gospel of John* (NIC; Grand Rapids: Wm. B. Eerdmans, 1971); and

15.22 R. Schnackenburg, *The Gospel According to St John;* Vol. I: *Introduction and Commentary on Chapters 1-4* (trans. K. Smyth; Herder's Theological Commentary on the New Testament; New York: Herder and Herder, 1968).

## Acts

15.23 F. F. Bruce, *The Acts of the Apostles: The Greek Text with Introduction and Commentary* (2nd ed.; Grand Rapids: Wm. B. Eerdmans, 1952 [see also F. F. Bruce, *Commentary on the Book of Acts: The English Text with Introduction, Exposition and Notes* (NIC; Grand Rapids: Wm. B. Eerdmans, 1954)] )—with Haenchen (15.24) and Lake and Cadbury (15.26) an excellent collection for this book;

15.24 E. Haenchen, *The Acts of the Apostles: A Commentary* (trans. B. Noble, G. Shinn, H. Anderson and R. McL. Wilson; Philadelphia: Westminster, 1971)—(see 15.23);

15.25 R. P. C. Hanson, *The Acts in the Revised Standard Version with Introduction and*

*Commentary* (The New Clarendon Bible [New Testament]; Oxford: Clarendon, 1967);

15.26 K. Lake and H. J. Cadbury, *English Translation and Commentary*, Vol. IV of *The Beginnings of Christianity*, Part I: *The Acts of the Apostles* (ed. F. J. Foakes Jackson and K. Lake; London: Macmillan, 1933; repr. Grand Rapids: Baker, 1965)—(see 15.23); and

15.27 C. S. C. Williams, *A Commentary on the Acts of the Apostles* (HNTC; New York: Harper and Brothers, 1957).

### Romans

15.28 C. K. Barrett, *A Commentary on the Epistle to the Romans* (HNTC; New York: Harper and Brothers, 1957);

15.29 F. F. Bruce, *The Epistle of Paul to the Romans: An Introduction and Commentary* (TNTC; Grand Rapids: Wm. B. Eerdmans, 1963);

15.30 F. J. Leenhardt, *The Epistle to the Romans: A Commentary* (trans. H. Knight; Cleveland and New York: World, 1961);

15.31 J. Murray, *The Epistle to the Romans: The English Text with Introduction, Exposition and Notes* (2 vols.; NIC; Grand Rapids: Wm. B. Eerdmans, 1960, 1965; also bound as 1 vol.); and

15.32 W. Sanday and A. C. Headlam, *A Critical and Exegetical Commentary on the Epistle to the Romans* (5th ed.; ICC; Edinburgh: T. & T. Clark, 1902).

### 1 Corinthians

15.33 C. K. Barrett, *A Commentary on the First Epistle to the Corinthians* (HNTC; New York: Harper and Row, 1968);

15.34 F. F. Bruce, *1 and 2 Corinthians* (New Century Bible; London: Oliphants, 1971);

15.35 J. Héring, *The First Epistle of Saint Paul to the Corinthians* (trans. A. W. Heathcote and P. J. Allcock; London: Epworth, 1962); and

15.36 A. Robertson and A. Plummer, *A Critical and Exegetical Commentary on the First Epistle of St Paul to the Corinthians* (2nd ed.; ICC; Edinburgh: T. & T. Clark, 1914).

## 2 Corinthians

F. F. Bruce (see 15.34);

15.37 J. Héring, *The Second Epistle of Saint Paul to the Corinthians* (trans. A. W. Heathcote and P. J. Allcock; London: Epworth, 1967);

15.38 P. Hughes, *Paul's Second Epistle to the Corinthians: The English Text with Introduction, Exposition and Notes* (NIC; Grand Rapids: Wm. B. Eerdmans, 1961); and

15.39 A. Plummer, *A Critical and Exegetical Commentary on the Second Epistle of St Paul to the Corinthians* (ICC; Edinburgh: T. & T. Clark, 1915).

## Galatians

15.40 E. D. Burton, *A Critical and Exegetical Commentary on the Epistle to the Galatians* (ICC; Edinburgh: T. & T. Clark, 1921)—a very fine commentary;

15.41 G. S. Duncan, *The Epistle of Paul to the Galatians* (MNTC; New York: Harper and Brothers, 1934);

15.42 D. Guthrie, *Galatians* (The Century Bible, New Series; London: Thomas Nelson, 1969); and

15.43 J. B. Lightfoot, *St. Paul's Epistle to the Galatians: A Revised Text with Introduction, Notes, and Dissertations* (19th ed.;

London: Macmillan, 1896; repr. Grand Rapids: Zondervan, 1957).

## Ephesians

15.44 T. K. Abbott, *A Critical and Exegetical Commentary on the Epistles to the Ephesians and to the Colossians* (ICC; Edinburgh: T. & T. Clark, 1897);

15.45 J. A. Robinson, *Saint Paul's Epistle to the Ephesians: A Revised Text and Translation, with Exposition and Notes* (2nd ed.; London: Macmillan, 1904); and

15.46 B. F. Westcott, *Saint Paul's Epistle to the Ephesians: The Greek Text with Notes and Addenda* (ed. J. M. Schulhof; London: Macmillan, 1906; repr. Grand Rapids: Wm. B. Eerdmans).

## Philippians

15.47 F. W. Beare, *A Commentary on the Epistle to the Philippians* (HNTC; New York: Harper and Row, 1959);

15.48 J. B. Lightfoot, *St. Paul's Epistle to the Philippians: A Revised Text with Introduction, Notes and Dissertations* (4th ed.; London: Macmillan, 1878; repr. Grand Rapids: Zondervan, 1953);

15.49 R. P. Martin, *The Epistle of Paul to the Philippians: An Introduction and Commentary* (TNTC; Grand Rapids: Wm. B. Eerdmans, 1959); and

15.50 M. R. Vincent, *A Critical and Exegetical Commentary on the Epistles to the Philippians and to Philemon* (ICC; Edinburgh: T. & T. Clark, 1897).

## Colossians

15.51 F. F. Bruce, *Commentary on the Epistle to the Colossians: The English Text with Intro-*

duction, *Exposition and Notes* (NIC; Grand Rapids: Wm. B. Eerdmans, 1957)—bound with E. K. Simpson on Ephesians;

15.52 J. B. Lightfoot, *St. Paul's Epistles to the Colossians and to Philemon: A Revised Text, with Introductions, Notes and Dissertations* (3rd ed.; London: Macmillan, 1879; repr. Grand Rapids: Zondervan, 1959);

15.53 E. Lohse, *Colossians and Philemon: A Commentary on the Epistles to the Colossians and to Philemon* (trans. W. R. Poehlmann and R. J. Karris; ed. H. Koester; Hermeneia; Philadelphia: Fortress, 1971)—a very fine commentary; and

15.54 C. F. D. Moule, *The Epistles of Paul the Apostle to the Colossians and to Philemon: An Introduction and Commentary* (Cambridge Greek Testament Commentary; Cambridge: University Press, 1957).

### 1 and 2 Thessalonians

15.55 J. E. Frame, *A Critical and Exegetical Commentary on the Epistles of St. Paul to the Thessalonians* (ICC; Edinburgh: T. & T. Clark, 1912);

15.56 G. Milligan, *St. Paul's Epistles to the Thessalonians: The Greek Text with Introduction and Notes* (London: Macmillan, 1908; repr. Grand Rapids: Wm. B. Eerdmans, 1952);

15.57 L. Morris, *The First and Second Epistles to the Thessalonians: The English Text with Introduction, Exposition and Notes* (NIC; Grand Rapids: Wm. B. Eerdmans, 1959); and

15.58 D. E. H. Whiteley, *Thessalonians in the Revised Standard Version with Introduction and Commentary* (The New Clarendon Bible [New Testament]; Oxford: University Press, 1969).

## 1 and 2 Timothy and Titus

15.59 C. K. Barrett, *The Pastoral Epistles in the New English Bible with Introduction and Commentary* (The New Clarendon Bible [New Testament]; Oxford: Clarendon, 1963);

15.60 M. Dibelius and H. Conzelmann, *The Pastoral Epistles: A Commentary on the Pastoral Epistles* (trans. P. Buttolph and A. Yarbro; ed. H. Koester; Hermeneia; Philadelphia: Fortress, 1972)—a very fine commentary;

15.61 D. Guthrie, *The Pastoral Epistles: An Introduction and Commentary* (TNTC; Grand Rapids: Wm. B. Eerdmans, 1957);

15.62 J. N. D. Kelly, *A Commentary on the Pastoral Epistles: I Timothy, II Timothy, Titus* (HNTC; New York: Harper and Row, 1963)—a very fine commentary; and

15.63 W. Lock, *A Critical and Exegetical Commentary on the Pastoral Epistles (I. & II. Timothy and Titus)* (ICC; Edinburgh: T. & T. Clark, 1924).

## Philemon

J. B. Lightfoot (see 15.52);

E. Lohse (see 15.53);

C. F. D. Moule (see 15.54); and

M. R. Vincent (see 15.50).

## Hebrews

15.64 F. F. Bruce, *The Epistle to the Hebrews: The English Text with Introduction, Exposition and Notes* (NIC; Grand Rapids: Wm. B. Eerdmans, 1964);

15.65 J. Héring, *The Epistle to the Hebrews* (trans. A. W. Heathcote and P. J. Allcock; London: Epworth, 1970);

15.66 J. Moffatt, *A Critical and Exegetical Commentary on the Epistle to the Hebrews* (ICC; Edinburgh: T. & T. Clark, 1924);

15.67 H. W. Montefiore, *A Commentary on the Epistle to the Hebrews* (HNTC; New York: Harper and Row, 1964); and

15.68 B. F. Westcott, *The Epistle to the Hebrews: The Greek Text with Notes and Essays* (3rd ed.; London: Macmillan, 1920; repr. Grand Rapids: Wm. B. Eerdmans).

### James

15.69 J. B. Mayor, *The Epistle of St. James: The Greek Text with Introduction, Notes and Comments* (3rd ed.; London: Macmillan, 1910);

15.70 C. L. Mitton, *The Epistle of James* (Grand Rapids: Wm. B. Eerdmans, 1966); and

15.71 J. H. Ropes, *A Critical and Exegetical Commentary on the Epistle of St. James* (ICC; Edinburgh: T. & T. Clark, 1916).

### 1 Peter

15.72 F. W. Beare, *The First Epistle of Peter: The Greek Text with Introduction and Notes* (3rd ed.; Oxford: Basil Blackwell, 1970);

15.73 C. A. Bigg, *A Critical and Exegetical Commentary on the Epistles of St. Peter and St. Jude* (2d ed.; ICC; Edinburgh: T. & T. Clark, 1902).

15.74 J. N. D. Kelly, *A Commentary on the Epistles of Peter and Jude* (HNTC; New York: Harper and Row, 1969); and

15.75 E. G. Selwyn, *The First Epistle of St. Peter: The Greek Text with Introduction, Notes and Essays* (2nd ed.; London: Macmillan/ New York: St. Martin's, 1947)—an excellent commentary.

## 2 Peter

C. A. Bigg (see 15.73);

15.76 M. Green, *The Second Epistle General of Peter and the General Epistle of Jude: An Introduction and Commentary* (TNTC; Grand Rapids: Wm B. Eerdmans, 1968);

J. N. D. Kelly (see 15.74); and

15.77 J. B. Mayor, *The Epistle of St. Jude and the Second Epistle of St. Peter: Greek Text with Introduction, Notes and Comments* (London: Macmillan, 1907; repr. Grand Rapids: Baker, 1965)—an extensive and good commentary.

## 1, 2 and 3 John

15.78 A. E. Brooke, *A Critical and Exegetical Commentary on the Johannine Epistles* (ICC; Edinburgh: T. & T. Clark, 1912);

15.79 F. F. Bruce, *The Epistles of John: Introduction, Exposition and Notes* (Old Tappan, New Jersey: Fleming H. Revell, 1970);

15.80 C. H. Dodd, *The Johannine Epistles* (MNTC; London: Hodder and Stoughton, 1946);

15.81 R. Law, *The Tests of Life: A Study of the First Epistle of St. John* (3rd ed.; Edinburgh: T. & T. Clark, 1914; repr. Grand Rapids: Baker, 1968)—a very fine study;

15.82 B. F. Westcott, *The Epistles of St John: The Greek Text with Notes and Essays* (4th ed.; London: Macmillan, 1902; repr., with an introduction by F. F. Bruce, Grand Rapids: Wm. B. Eerdmans, 1966).

## Jude

C. A. Bigg (see 15.73);

M. Green (see 15.76);

J. N. D. Kelly (see 15.74); and

J. B. Mayor (see 15.77).

# Revelation

15.83 I. T. Beckwith, *The Apocalypse of John: Studies in Introduction, with a Critical and Exegetical Commentary* (New York: Macmillan, 1919; repr. Grand Rapids: Baker, 1967)—a very fine study;

15.84 G. B. Caird, *A Commentary on the Revelation of St. John the Divine* (HNTC; New York: Harper and Row, 1966);

15.85 R. H. Charles, *A Critical and Exegetical Commentary on the Revelation of St. John with Introduction, Notes and Indices, also the Greek Text and English Translation* (2 vols.; ICC; Edinburgh: T. & T. Clark, 1920)—an excellent collection of important data;

15.86 G. E. Ladd, *A Commentary on the Revelation of John* (Grand Rapids: Wm. B. Eerdmans, 1972); and

15.87 H. B. Swete, *The Apocalypse of St John: The Greek Text with Introduction, Notes and Indices* (3rd ed.; London: Macmillan, 1908; repr. Grand Rapids: Wm. B. Eerdmans, 1951).

Chapter Sixteen

# Interpretive Principles for
# New Testament Exegesis

The use of the reference works in this guide involves
some knowledge of the principles of the interpretation of
the New Testament, including the data both of hermeneutics and hermeneutic.

A good beginning would be in a knowledge of the
history of biblical interpretation (see also 8.4 and 8.5):

>16.1 R. M. Grant, *A Short History of the Inter-
>pretation of the Bible* (rev. ed.; New York:
>Macmillan, 1963).

From the several books on interpretive principles the
following few (plus two articles) should prove to be
helpful both in terms of procedures and in terms of
questions to be confronted (see also, of course, Danker):

>16.2 C. E. Braaten, *History and Hermeneutics*
>(New Directions in Theology Today, Vol. II;
>Philadelphia: Westminster, 1966);

>16.3 W. G. Doty, *Contemporary New Testament
>Interpretation* (Englewood Cliffs: Prentice-
>Hall, 1972);

>16.4 R. W. Funk, *Language, Hermeneutic and
>Word of God: The Problem of Language in
>the New Testament and Contemporary The-
>ology* (New York: Harper and Row, 1966);

16.5  E. Krentz, *Biblical Studies Today: A Guide to Current Issues and Trends* (Biblical Monographs; St. Louis: Concordia, 1966);

16.6  E. Krentz, "A Survey of Trends and Problems in Biblical Interpretation," *Concordia Theological Monthly* 40 (1969), 276-93;

16.7  G. E. Ladd, *The New Testament and Criticism* (Grand Rapids: Wm. B. Eerdmans, 1967);

16.8  A. B. Mickelsen, *Interpreting the Bible* (Grand Rapids: Wm. B. Eerdmans, 1963);

16.9  J. Reumann, "Methods in Studying the Biblical Text Today," *Concordia Theological Monthly* 40 (1969), 655-81;

16.10 J. M. Robinson and J. B. Cobb, Jr., *The New Hermeneutic* (New Frontiers in Theology, Vol. II; New York: Harper and Row, 1964); and

16.11 K. Stendahl, *The Bible and the Role of Women: A Case Study in Hermeneutics* (trans. E. T. Sander; Facet Books, Biblical Series—15; Philadelphia: Fortress, 1966).

# Author Index

[The numbers refer to bibliographic entries]

Abbott, T. K. 15.44
Ackroyd, P. R. 14.2
Adcock, F. E. 11.19
Aharoni, Y. 9.1, 9.10
Aland, K. 3.1, 3.2, 3.8, 3.9
Albright, W. F. 9.3, 9.6
Aldrich, E. V. 1.9
Allen, W. C. 15.5
Alsop, J. R. 6.17
Altaner, B. 13.32
Armerding, C. E. 1.7
Armstrong, A. H. 11.22, 11.23
Arndt, W. F. 6.1, 6.17, 15.13
Avi-Yonah, M. 9.1, 9.11

Baillie, J. 13.24
Baly, D. 9.2, 9.12
Banks, A. 9.7
Barber, E. A. 6.5
Barclay, W. 14.11
Barker, E. 11.1
Barnes, D. H. 6.12
Barns, J. W. B. 13.12
Baron, S. W. 12.1
Barrett, C. K. 11.2, 15.18, 15.28, 15.33, 15.59
Bauer, W. 6.1, 6.17
Baumgartner, W. 6.21, 6.22, 6.23, 6.24
Baynes, N. H. 11.19

Beare, F. W. 15.47, 15.72
Beck, W. F. 14.12
Beckwith, I. T. 15.83
Behm, J. 8.2
Berlin, C. 2.20
Bettenson, H. 13.2
Bickerman, E. J. 8.18, 11.15, 11.16
Bigg, C. A. 15.73
Black, M. 3.2, 15.1
Blackman, P. 12.33
Blass, F. 7.1
Blau, J. L. 12.1
Bonnet, M. 13.15
Bowker, J. 12.29
Box, G. H. 12.40, 12.46
Braaten, C. E. 16.1, 16.2
Bratcher, R. G. 14.13
Braude, W. G. 12.42, 12.43
Briggs, C. A. 6.20
Broadribb, D. 2.21
Brooke, A. E. 4.5, 15.78
Brown, F. 6.20
Brown, R. E. 15.2, 15.19
Bruce, F. F. 8.15, 14.1, 14.14, 15.23, 15.29, 15.34, 15.51, 15.64, 15.79, 15.82
Bultmann, R. 8.8, 15.20
Burchard, C. 2.11, 2.12
Burich, N. J. 2.23

89

90

91

92

94